WAS I A POET

AND DIDN'T KNOW IT?

Basic Wisdom for Dumb Rednecks

By Richard L. Folsom

JRW PUBLISHING
4415-C Constitution Lane
Marianna, Florida 32448
(850) 693-0605

Was I a Poet and Didn't Know It?

Copyright © 2007 by Richard L. Folsom

Originally published in comb binder in 2007 by Richard L. Folsom

All rights reserved. This book or any of its parts may not be copied or used in any way without written permission of Richard L. Folsom, c/o JRW Publishing, 4415C Constitution Lane, Marianna, Florida 32448.

Was I a Poet is a two-volume book, with *Was I an Author* being the second volume, and both are included in the reserved rights.

Portions of this book have been registered with the Library of Congress under Form #SRu647-607 for sound recording, United States Copyright Office. Registration for the remaining portion has been applied for at the United States Library of Congress Copyright Office.

Cover canoe photograph by Foster "Shag" Willis of Marianna, Florida.

Picture of the author was taken by Hayes Baggett of Marianna, Florida.

Cover design by Judy Williams, JRW Publishing of Marianna, Florida.

ISBN: 978-0-9826678-0-4

For information regarding special discounts for bulk purchases, please contact JRW Publishing Sales at 1-850-693-0605 or jrwpublishing@yahoo.com.

TABLE OF CONTENTS

Acknowledgement………………………………....…	4
Disclaimer…………………………………………..	5
About the Author………………………………....	6
You Can Be……………………………………...	8
Introduction………………………………………..	9
Just a Thought…………………………………...	11
Chapter One – Before the Beginning……….....……	13
Chapter Two – A Happy Song…………………….	23
Trees……………………………………………...	24
Eugene's Poem…………………………………...	25
A Happy Song…………………………………...	26
Chapter Three – Figure It Out…………………….	31
Figure It Out……………………………………...	32
Chapter Four – Sandbar Saturday Night……....……	59
Talkin' Walkin'…………………………………...	59
Sandbar Saturday Night…………………………..	61
Chapter Five – TV Analogy………………………..	69
TV Analogy……………………………………...	70
Chapter Six – Different Ways of Looking at the Same Thing………………………………………..	83
Different Ways of Looking at the Same Thing…………..	86
Chapter Seven – How to Do It…………………….	95

ACKNOWLEDGEMENT

I want to dedicate this book to Jan, my friend and companion and inspiration. A perfect example of what a human being should be. She took care of me without a single complaint when I was unable to care for myself. Without her love I would not have been able to, or known how, to write this book. God Bless You.

DISCLAIMER

Before you read a single word in this book, please be warned that all the ideas and views in this book are going to appear very, very radical to probably most of the information you have stored on theology, mental health, government, business, and education. I don't claim to be a qualified advisor on any of them. The book is simply my own personal opinion of these things and is mentioned simply for food for thought for the reader to examine and form his own opinions. If you don't feel competent on your own to examine this material, please discuss it with your mental health provider, spiritual advisor, lawyer, or teacher and get their permission to take responsibility for reading the ideas presented here and you do so at your own risk. I know that there will be some people who will strongly disagree with my conclusions, but I don't see how they can argue if they investigate the differences of our opinions with an open mind. It works for me. I had to add this part for my protection from a lawsuit.

ABOUT THE AUTHOR

I wasn't an author or poet before writing this book and I still may not be, because it doesn't follow the established rules of writing. I wrote this book for me anyway and I make up my own rules in life, which separates me from most of the dummies I know. So that is all the authority I need to present it to the public.

I'm going to be covering some information that will be familiar to some and foreign to others. Some is new information and some has been around forever. I'm going to talk about things we have been conditioned not to argue about which has led humanity on a wild goose chase for happiness. I'm going to tell you why you aren't happy and how to get that way.

Most books on this subject were written by very qualified and educated people usually with a specific background in the theme of their work, but generally they are not speaking the language of a large group of people out there. I'm talking about common people in factories, honky-tonks, sports arenas, 18-wheelers, hunting camps, on construction sites, farm tractors, fishing boats as well as many housewives raising our kids. Lots of these people are not educated in or concerned about, most of the breakthroughs in modern research and technology in every aspect you care to consider, and are unaware of the implications of that knowledge. The dummies who haven't been keeping up with what is going on are going to be shocked to find out that reality is not real, and this whole world is not anything like what it seems to be. I think I understand what the intellectuals know and I'm going to attempt to condense and organize it and translate it to country-boy lingo. I've used every cliché I know and have tried to use simple concepts anyone can understand.

My formal education includes high school, a little college and several trade schools, which help me understand the group I'm trying to reach. Don't get me wrong, there are lots of educated, sophisticated, and wealthy dummies out there also and they are welcome to read my book, but I am a redneck fisherman who has done mostly electrical construction for the past 35 years and I might not speak their language.

All it takes to be a dummy is to think that you will ever locate and capture real happiness in the world of ego consciousness. You can not satisfy an ego and it will always want more and more. The key to happiness is wanting less and less and the definition of happiness is being satisfied without anything. Believe it or not, everything you will ever need is already yours, but it is only located in your spiritual consciousness. The purpose of this book is to show you that and how to go about accessing that spiritual area and how to avoid the trauma of ego consciousness.

My goal is to point out to anyone interested, an explanation of how humans with all their ego-motivated behaviors and social orders and governments and religions have led us to the present world situation and what you as an individual can do about it. Just because you are stuck in the chaos and insanity of the collective consciousness' physical and material world that your body was born into, does not justify continuing to waste your energy there. You were born into a spiritual world long before that and can re-enter that world of love and peace and happiness simply by investing your energy in spiritual consciousness.

You must first understand though, that ego and spirit are on opposite ends of your path and that any movement toward one is also a movement away from the other. It doesn't take a genius to figure out that if you are not happy, then you have been heading the wrong way.

My real education comes from a lifetime of searching for the truth, so although I do not guarantee the accuracy of every single item in this book, because most of it was taken from other so-called experts in their field or from my memory, I do guarantee that the overall conclusions I draw are true and can be validated by you or anyone else who is willing to invest the energy to subdue ego and pursue spiritual consciousness.

YOU CAN BE

You can be happy or you can be sad.
You can be satisfied or you can be mad.
You can be good or you can be bad.
You can have or you can be had.
It's up to you, what are you going to do.
Just trust in the Lord and He'll pull you through.
There's no need to worry no need to be blue
Just love everybody is all you've got to do.
Makes no difference what you have been.
He'll stick with you through thick and thin.
All you have to do is look within
And you will find the Lord where he's always been.
He's in the sky, and He's in the sea.
He's in the forest in every tree.
He's in the bird, and He's in the bee.
He's in you, and He's in me.

You can be up or you can be down.
You can wear a smile or you can wear a frown.
You can be lost or you can be found.
You can be up tight or you can clown around.
It's up to you what are you going to be
Trust in the Lord and He will set you free.
He's everywhere its plain to see
And He'll be there with you through Eternity.
Makes no difference what you have been.
He'll stick with you through thick and thin.
All you have to do is look within
And you'll find the Lord where He's always been.
He's in the sky, and He's in the sea.
He's in the forest in every tree.
He's in the bird; He's in the bee.
He's in you, and He's in me.

INTRODUCTION

That little poem came in to my attention out of the clear blue sky one day while I was painting my canoe. By the time I finished painting the canoe I had also finished writing the poem which came as if it had been dictated from another dimension of my consciousness, unsolicited, in rhyme, in order and completed.

By then, I had already received several poems or songs in the same way and I was trying to write a brief explanation of this brand new phenomenon that had just started showing up in my life. After three or four attempts, I realized that it couldn't be done briefly so I compiled my earlier attempts into this book which all started one day when, for the first time, I tried to write a happy song for my own amusement.

I needed some happy thoughts real bad. I was recovering from a fall that had shattered both feet. I spent months in pain in a recliner chair unable to hardly go anywhere or do anything. I was already pretty happy after 50 years of trying and practicing to be. I had worked hard to be in control of my life and my thoughts, and I saw this unfortunate accident as an opportunity to polish up my spirit and to erase my ego. After a while, I must have established a connection with my higher consciousness because it began to write poems and songs and probably most of the information in this book for me. It is not real common but there have been many people who have channeled information in many different ways, all at least very interesting, and some downright fascinating.

I was fascinated at the information I was receiving and how I was receiving it. I have never cared much for poetry because I could never seem to understand what other people thought it meant, so I probably know less about poetry than anything else. Until a few months ago, if anyone had asked what the last thing I was likely to do in the world; my truest answer could have been to write poetry. I still can't do it on my own, but some of the stuff that has come through me after maybe making a suggestion of a topic or theme, is for me the real stuff. I'm usually more surprised by its contents than anyone, and I'm pretty familiar with my thoughts and I know some of this is not coming from in here. Was I a poet in another life or is my guardian angel a poet or did I tap into the big Internet in the sky or is that just God's way of sending messages? I don't know.

I'm probably just smart enough to be dangerous. Most of my education came from the school of hard knocks and on my own, so it is therefore considerably different from someone whose curriculum was dictated by a government-subsidized university with mandatory classes. I tried to filter out the bullshit as I learned and each thing led to another until I had learned at least a little bit about everything that I felt was important in relation to the human condition. The more you learn, the more you find that there are things you don't know anything about, and so I know so much that I know that I don't know much at all. But, I do know that I am not my body and that is all you need to know to kick ego's ass out of control of your body and allow your spirit to take you to happiness. It may take hundreds of years, if we have that long, at the rate we are going, but I hope that my poem, *Happy Song*, will finally one day be understood by everybody along with *TV Analogy* and *Different Ways of Looking at the Same Thing*. My poem, *Sandbar Saturday Night*, can be understood now by fishermen and non-fishermen alike but the non-fisherman is going to have to go fishing one time to experience it, unless he can do it in a dream. Watching it on TV or reading about it in a magazine counts about as much as watching General Hospital because you are sick.

If the non-fisherman realizes that practically every line of that poem contains vital information in stalking a catfish and if that information is correctly understood and applied, then he will become a fisherman because he will catch fish. That is the same way I feel about *Happy Song* and *TV Analogy*. If you fish for happiness you can catch it. If you want to go flying around the universe, you can do that too, but you'll have to leave ego at the house.

This world is nothing like the world we grew up in. Every day, scientists in every field are publishing new findings on new information that radically opposes the views we once held on reality. They have studied everything that has been found in the universe and their investigation has revealed just how dumb most of humanity really is. My goal is to help you to understand this.

This next little poem came to me one morning as I was on the final re-write of this book and it is basically the message I would like to share with everyone.

JUST A THOUGHT

You'll never see me without a smile
I put it on in the morning and wear it for a while
I have to take it off though every now and then
It's hard to go for long without wearing my grin
It's been this way since I found out
Just exactly what life is all about
All you have to do is just do your best
And trust your higher self and it will do the rest
Every single thing begins with a thought
The life you are living is what they brought
If you find that things are not going your way
Realize that your future is constructed every day
You already know what you've done wrong
Put out some good vibrations and it won't be very long
You'll be happy too and everything will be all right
You'll be through with darkness you will see the light.

CHAPTER ONE
BEFORE THE BEGINNING

Some of my earliest memories of childhood are of changing from pajamas to Sunday-Go-To-Meeting clothes, then into play clothes, then back into Sunday clothes for evening services, then back into play clothes until pajama time again. Between that and not being allowed to go fishing on Sunday and spending the first week of every summer vacation in Bible School, although I did thank God for the Kool-Aid and sweet cookies they served that helped me get through, my appetite for religion was curbed pretty early.

I only lived a few blocks from the church so I had to show up nearly every time they opened the doors. I did enjoy the music and singing and still do. Even way back then, although I couldn't express it, I didn't think they understood all they knew about what they were trying to teach me. As I got older and began to notice behavior, too many of them seemed to act as if they believed they could behave in their personal or business life anyway they pleased, as long as they didn't say any bad words or drink liquor in public and showed up Sunday with their offering, to agree that Jesus had bought them a ticket to Heaven. I had the notion that Jesus had come to point the way to the ticket booth and to teach us how to raise our own fare. His teachings were very simple and all of them were directed at choosing spiritual consciousness over ego consciousness and can be summed up by the Golden Rule.

We have two eyes, two ears, two arms, two legs, and two hemispheres of the brain. It's not hard to believe that we have two types of consciousness. I will be using the term spirit to refer to that level of consciousness that is indeed spirit or energy that transcends physical form. That is the part of you that is connected to the rest of the energy of the universe, which I think is the best definition of God, as if a human could actually reduce that energy to words. We are only human beings because we vibrate at the human frequency of universal energy that existed before our bodies were born and will still be here when our bodies die. It is also here now, but most people spend most of their lifetime unaware of its presence due to the overwhelming presence of the body's ego consciousness, which I will refer to as ego. Ego is the body's read out of sensory data as perceived and run through the mind. It's the part of you that will do almost anything to maintain its individual identity, while striving to be just like the rest of the egos. It's the part you refer to when you say the devil made me do that. The mind creates the body while the body is creating the mind. So out of just this small portion of the total spectrum of energy, it is the only place that they exist. So all the ideas you have ever had that are ego based are no longer valid when you are no longer in the body's ego consciousness, through death, dreams, trance, meditation, hypnosis, coma, or miracle. How else are you going to explain Peter walking on water, or dreams about flying, or past life experiences, or near death phenomena, or UFO abductions or ghosts, or extra sensory perception, or astrology, or communicating with the dead, or astral projection? That is too big of a pile to sweep under the carpet. These issues have to be addressed. You may say God did it and you may be right, but understanding more about how it was done will help you to understand why and will enable you to make more intelligent decisions about life. Why is easy, because we are all component parts of the whole thing, so it makes sense to love thy neighbor as thy self because he is you on the spiritual level of consciousness. Your ego might not believe that and could get you into lots of trouble, but it doesn't care, because it knows that it has a death sentence hanging over its head anyway. Your spirit though, is going to be here a while. Don't forget yin and yang or what you sow you shall reap. Don't let your ego run your battery down or you may have to go through hell to get a jump start. If a word can offend you, you've got a long way to go, and you're going to have a hell of a time finishing this book. So I will help you now to get over it now. Because of the slow learning process from infancy through childhood and puberty into adults, our minds have been pumped so full of bullshit that it is okay to be ignorant, but to stay ignorant is the greatest sin, (Gospel according to Richard). There you have it. If you don't, and if words still have power over your feelings, you need to stop here and figure out why. Has your brain been so thoroughly washed that it can accept B.S., or bull-caca, or bull number two, or bovine excrement when it expresses the same thought. Did you ever notice how certain words have become forbidden yet in order to forbid them they can be substituted by a letter and are perfectly appropriate (i.e., n-word, f-word, b-word, etc.)? What about substituting a similar word such as heck or darn or biscuit-eater? They mean the same but it is not the thought, but your reaction to it that counts. It only has the power that you want to invest in it. What a trivial thing to waste your power on. But that is ego's job, wasting energy, or so it thinks.

An old friend of mine who's ego finally pushed him to the gates of Hell "found the Lord" and started going to church and studying the Bible. He accidentally paid me the best compliment I have ever received when one day he told me that he was going to lead a Bible study at his church. He paused a moment when he saw the big smile on my face, then he added that I probably wouldn't fit in because everybody thinks I'm crazy as Hell. Hallelujah, at least everybody sees the difference between me and all the rest, but who is really the craziest? None of the people I know can truthfully say these things about themselves. I'm happy. I don't worry. I'm responsible. I'm not afraid of anything, including death or disaster. I'm not greedy, or jealous, or prejudiced. I don't care for material things or possessions. I'm honest, considerate, compassionate, generous and loving. I'm in direct control of my life and not indebted to anyone. I work when I want to and play when I want to. I am not intimidated by anyone. I don't give a shit what anyone on the planet thinks about me because most of them really are certifiably crazy. When I need anything it usually just shows up and at the right time. I wouldn't be paranoid if everyone wasn't out to get me! It has taken over thirty years of hard work to get this crazy.

Although it could happen, don't count on dethroning the ego overnight. The longer it has been running wild, the harder it is to subdue. It will probably take a long time just to realize just how dumb you really are, but that is the first step. Your ego knows all the tricks and has probably heard enough of this bullshit and wants you to throw down this book and go shopping or something. Well, you can shop till you drop but you cannot purchase, at any price, the feelings you have when you enter the spiritual consciousness. That scares the shit out of ego, because it knows when you find that out, the party is over. It is for the ego, but the real party is just beginning, and the sky is the limit, if you need limits. It is actually just that simple.

If you are not crazy yet, just keep reading, and I can damn near guarantee you will be by the time you finish or at least you will know how to be. It has always been your choice and you are the result of all your choices. Do your own inventory of ego motivated paths you have taken and see where they have led you. I rest my case.

One more thing about words, I have used the word Hell, so let me clear this subject up for you now. Since Hell implies the devil let me begin with him. Think about this...One day I went into the intensive care unit to see my Mom. She was not only terminally ill with liver problems, but she had fallen and broken her arm and hip socket. Needless to say, she was drugged to the max. I knew she had been floating in and out of her body consciousness because she could accurately describe things going on in the adjoining rooms which were only glassed into the nurses' station, but not to the adjacent rooms. She said that she could see through the solid walls. She also said that she had seen the devil and he had been sitting over the doorsill watching her. My Mother was a very religious woman and church member for seventy plus years where she had heard a lot about God and the devil. Now hear this! She said that he looked just like his picture. As far as I know, no one has a photograph of the devil or I would have heard about it by now. I don't think he has sat for any portraits either. Over the ages, artists have drawn or created pictures of the devil in thousands of different looks. Now here is the question. Did my Mom happen to see the only real devil's picture, out of the thousands possible or did the devil that was created in the picture become the devil in my Mom's room? I have to say yes to the latter because it was a thought form and in the out-of-body consciousness-state she was in, it was real. So be careful what thought forms you let into your mind. You might see them again. It's the same way with Hell. If you are expecting a mountain of fire, that is what you might get. However, the real Hell can be right here on Earth and a lot of people can attest to that. Negative actions cause negative consequences. Look around and check out the conditions of some people's life.

    This can also be a Heaven on Earth and I think I have figured out this "streets paved with gold" thing. Too bad ego, it is not real gold, and it is not just the streets. On a few occasions, I have experienced spiritual consciousness to the degree at which I became aware of my connection to everything else. At this time, a golden light permeates everything. Because of the intensely wonderful feelings of this state, it is no doubt identified as Heaven, and it is located at the other end of the energy spectrum, the one that ego keeps off limits, through its consumption of your energy. You don't have to wait until you die to experience Heaven or Hell. You have the equipment and you can learn to use it now. That is what life is about.

    There are plenty of teachers out there of all kinds and basically they are all talking about the same thing. Don't believe any of them, especially if they charge a fee, until you check them out for yourself. First you must open up your mind and clear out the bullshit very carefully. Then check out the facts and very soon certain truths will become visible and as you build on to these truths, they will create a new view of the world to guide you to happiness. It worked for me. I'm still learning every day and I just recently realized that your rate of growth is directly proportional to the amount of energy you spend on it. I will explain this fully later on, but now I want to tell you how I found out, and how I came to writing this book, and the poetry that this book is about.

I have been searching for the truth most of my life, covering a broad range of subject matter pertaining to all the different aspects of life. I think I know at least a little bit about almost everything that I consider important. I don't consider myself an expert at anything except maybe sniffing out bullshit, which I have been doing for over fifty years now. I've been on this path a long time and have had my share of backslides and periods when ego ran wild and I have been caught up in stressful situations but over all I have made some good progress

I never believed in working all your life so you can retire when you get old. I was always concerned that I may not get old, so I have always worked a while and took off a while, another one of my crazy traits. I was born poor and thank God I have managed to stay that way, but that has helped to make me wealthy beyond measure, because while all those egos are stacking up money and material things, I have been stacking up wisdom and knowledge, which lead to the real treasure.

I was on an extended vacation after a long and stressful job. I fully intended to catch up on some reading and studying and to work on getting my mind back into the right place. My ego was having so much fun running up and down that river, camping, fishing, swimming, and exploring that I failed to pay attention to my first decision, to not climb up that bank right there, but to go up river a little bit more where it would be much easier. I'm a little lazier than my buddy who had already navigated the six or seven foot vertical face with a crevice large enough to get in to climb. We were already about forty feet above the boat up a gradual forty-five degree sloping bank that had been undercut by the river revealing seashells packed in some places one hundred feet above river level. The shells had not been there long enough to turn to limestone and were very crumbly. I had already spent three or four days climbing around studying this place with no problems. In no way could you have convinced me that it was possible to fall more than six feet there if it was even possible to fall at all. That was the last thing on my mind as I re-decided to follow my buddy up the bank. I climbed about three steps up the inside of that crevice when the bank under my feet gave way. In one nanosecond, I was flying through the air face down over a field of strewn boulders from the size of a TV to the size of a refrigerator, made of pure shell. All I had on was some cut off shorts and diving shoes. I had enough time to say "Oh Shit," and pick out a smooth spot to land. Because of the years I had spent on the diving board at the pool as a kid, I was able to nail a perfect landing on the small smooth sand bed I chose about thirty-five feet below, but it was as hard as a rock. It did collapse under my left heel and bent that foot backward, breaking most of my toes and some bones in the top of that foot. I knew that my right heel bone was crushed, by the new ripples on both sides of my ankle. Every bone, ligament, tendon and muscle in all ten toes, both feet and ankles were broken or strained or pulled, or stretched. I had a bruise that ran from my right heel up the back of my leg to my crotch, but everything else seemed to work all right. I was lucky to be alive and not more seriously injured. Like most poor folks, I didn't have any insurance and was about out of money too. I have had enough broken bones over the years from sometimes pushing thresholds a little too far by living life to the max, that I knew there wasn't much a doctor could do that I couldn't. I'll spare you the details but after a couple of days I agreed to go to a doctor because my right ankle looked bad. There wasn't much he could do but he did confirm all the broken bones and said they were lined up good enough to leave them alone. I had not had a wink of sleep since the accident and there was no way to hold my feet that didn't hurt. He gave me the strongest pain medicine he could prescribe, the kind they give to dying cancer patients but it barely touched the pain. I remember telling a friend at the time that it hurt just as bad but didn't quite matter as much. Only a few days after my fall I got sick with a terrible stomachache and spent the whole day throwing up about once an hour. During all that heaving, my neck got somehow out of alignment, which caused the worst headache I've ever had. I was so sick I think I would have had to get better to die. I had so much pain coming in that my brain actually shut off my feet pain and kept it off most of that day until I started getting over the stomach and head and neck pain. Three different times that day I banged my feet on the floor just to be sure they didn't hurt. That was all I needed to know. I was determined to find that switch in my brain and turn that pain off for good. Pain is a great motivator when you have been slacking on controlling your thoughts. You can ride pain way deep into the darkest recesses of your mind. Many years ago, I had used the emotional pain of ending a long and mostly happy marriage the same way with great results. I had reached my mid-life crisis and just had to go. I used an old Indian Shaman's technique of sensory deprivation by burying myself in the ground for a few days with the intention of not coming out until I had resolved everything that was standing between me and happiness. That was the only way I could keep my ego from distracting me and putting off working on my spirit. A young psychologist I had seen on TV talking about how we're all full of erroneous ideas and how we need to go back through the filing cabinets of our mind and remove the junk, and reprogram our thoughts and take control of them. I not only read the books, but I applied them to my life. I'm not sure what all happened in that hole but the "me" who went in there was not the same as the one who came out. It was probably what Christians call the "Born Again Experience." To be born again implies that something has to die. That something is ego. So don't come around me in your flashy automobile with your designer jeans and gold and diamonds hanging off your liposuctioned ass and tell me you have been born again, or it might hurt your feelings when I tell you that you are full of shit. You can't worship two masters if they are on opposite ends of the same scale. Your preacher may say you are saved, but if he makes his living off of religion, he is selling you a product that he doesn't have to produce, and I hate to have to pop his bubble, but Jesus ain't for sale!

If you have ever stumped your toe, multiply that by about a million, and you will understand what I was experiencing, for several months non-stop. That's a lot of motivation. Let me rephrase what I said about killing off the ego. You don't want to actually kill the ego, just choke the son of a bitch down to his very last breath and then keep your hands on his throat because he will never quit trying to run the body. He will be satisfied to kill the body rather than give up control. It happens all the time. You can though, through will power take that control back from ego, by unlearning all the behavior patterns that put him in control, and by relearning to let spirit into the driver's seat.

I went into over drive erasing my ego. That recliner chair that almost grew to my ass became my new hole. Again, I went back through my mind tossing out junk, setting new priorities, doing my dreaming exercises, meditating, contemplating the universe, reading some new books and rereading some old books again. Day after day I invested all my energy toward spirit and gradually got away from pain and ego for longer and longer periods.

For recreation, I would get out my guitar and practice playing and singing the old country gospel songs I love so much. I don't care for new type gospel music filled with blood and crosses and worship and rulers and kings and mansions and the rest of the ego mentality words and phrases you hear over and over. The term Lord is about the only word normally used for universal almighty power, that doesn't conjure up for me, preconceived ideas of some old male human figure and all the rules He made to determine whether or not you have been selected to heaven or doomed to hell. There is a world of difference between there is one God and God is one, or made in His image and made of the same stuff. You can blame language for the maleness, since it was no doubt a male ego who attached that gender to the word.

In the little poem, *You Can Be*, that I opened this book with, and the poem, *Just a Thought*, which came to me one morning as I was beginning my next to final rewrite, I used the term Lord in one and higher self in the other, referring to the universal energy that resides in every part of the universe.

I didn't write a chapter about them and they are my idea of what a gospel song should be. They are self explanatory and simple enough for even a child to understand and they include all you need to know for success. I put them first to keep the poet critics and poem lovers interested long enough to get to my other poetry.

Although I'm so tone deaf I can't even tune my own guitar properly and even though I've been playing with it for years, I'm still in the beginner stage. I nearly twisted my birdie finger off years ago on a rope swing at the lake and it doesn't work just right, so I dropped out of guitar school on the forth string cause I couldn't make good, clear chords, but I did learn about ten notes on those four strings and they were enough for me to play about anything I could hum, one note at a time and in my key, whatever that is. My singing is even worse than my guitar playing, and to do both at the same time requires enough concentration to qualify it as yoga or some "not doing" exercise. The ego gets so caught up in combining the two activities that it shuts up the internal dialogue. So, even my recreation was spiritually oriented. After a while though, even I got tired of those same ten notes and dozen or so songs. One day I got to thinking about wanting to sing a happy song and could not think of any at the time. I figured, "Well, I'll just write a happy song 'cause I sure ain't going anywhere for a while." I got out a pencil and some paper and started thinking. After about an hour I didn't have a single word on that paper and worse still, did not even have a clue of an idea. I went on back to my old songs and never gave it another thought.

CHAPTER TWO
A HAPPY SONG

The very next morning after breakfast, I struggled into the wheelchair and wheeled out on the porch to soak up some sunshine. It was just a few months after the accident and I was just getting to where I could get in and out of the chair without hollering. I picked up my guitar on the way out but before I even reached the spot I usually sit, I asked my friend, Jan who was taking care of me, to bring me a pencil and paper. A whole chorus of a new song popped out of my mouth before she could even get there. It poured out like water from a pitcher and kept on coming out about as fast as I could write it down. In a couple of hours, I had three versus and two choruses totaling almost fifty lines. The next day, two more verses popped out, three or four lines at a time. I kept reading it over and over and changed places with verse two and three and combined verses four and five and added a word or two for clarity and decided it needed one more verse to tie it all together.

The next day I wrote the final verse, although it too seemed to just pop out. Jan asked me where I was going to get the music for it and I said, "It wrote itself, it will do the music too." It did just that. The rhythm of the words and phrases created its own music. I know less about music than I do about poetry and about the only thing I know about poetry is the term iambic pentameter, and I would not have known that if I hadn't had the best English teacher you can get in high school. She ran her class like a boot camp, but I can still remember trying to inform her that classical music sounded like cat's squalling and that rock and roll is where it's at.

I guess that it's because my Libra mind needs an encyclopedia of information on a subject before my scales will balance on an answer to even a simple question that I look at things from so many different points of view. I can read poetry or the

Bible, over and over and over and still not be sure I have a clue as to what they were talking about.

Therefore, any poetry or music coming from me is a miracle in itself, and if it doesn't rhyme, it ain't poetry to me, no matter who wrote it. You may have probably noticed by now that I'm no scholar or intellectual, but who is to say that a layman's opinion is not valid?

On only two other occasions have I ever attempted to write a poem or song or anything else. When I was in the sixth grade, every student in my grammar school was assigned to write a poem for Arbor Day, about trees. My poem was selected winner of the sixth grade and along with all the other grade winners I received a one dollar bill and lunch at the Woman's Club, where we each read our poem. This is the way I remember it.

TREES

> Some trees are big.
> Some trees are small.
> Some trees are short.
> Some trees are tall.
> Some trees are old.
> Some trees are young.
> Some trees are used
> for swings to be hung.

About thirty years later a friend of mine sent me an invitation to visit him and along with the letter he sent a picture of the stump end of a huge log across the creek that we had fished off of on a camping trip. He had glued a little picture of a frog to it and wrote a string of assorted words on the back of it. I'm sure he meant for it to be a poem but I never did figure out what in the hell he was talking about, so I hunted up a crazy picture that I had accidentally taken on the pier at the beach while trying to load the camera. It was an off angle view of about five or six oak plank boards from the walkway of the pier. I figured I'll just show him how to write a real poem so I spent the three hours of the trip to his house writing a poem on the back of that picture. Here is how I remember that poem. It didn't have a name so I will call it *Eugene's Poem*.

EUGENE'S POEM

I guess it all started
When a wind from the south
Blew an acorn from a tree
And it started to sprout.
It grew and grew
With it's friends and kin
Till it was cut down
By the lumber men.
Hauled down the highway
Chained to a truck
Took to the sawmill
And got all cut up.
Yeah that's me
I'm the third from the right.
I'm a little bit weathered
But my nails are still tight.
So if you are ever
At the Beach at P.C.
Come on by
And say howdy to me.

Now here is the *Happy Song* that started this whole thing.

A HAPPY SONG

You can get the blues by watching the news
And listening to all those points of views
Look at the world and try to guess
Just which part is in the biggest mess.
I don't care what the people say
About what is going on in the World today.
I think I've got it figured out.
Nobody really knows what they're talking about.
If you win in life or if you lose
It all depends on if you choose
To worry about what all is wrong
Or to sing yourself a Happy Song.
I'm going to sing me a Happy Song
And I'm going to sing it loud and strong.
I don't care what comes along.
I'm going to sing a Happy Song.

I can't control how other people feel
Or what they think about what is real.
There's a whole lot more to reality
Than the way we perceive what we hear, touch, and see.
Be it truth or myth or fiction
It's all just part of the description.
The description of the me I see
Is what forms this reality
So if I want to see a change
I'll just have to rearrange
The way I've been thinking all along
And choose to sing myself a Happy Song.
Well I'm going to sing me a Happy Song

And I'm going to sing it all day long.
It don't matter what all is wrong
I'll keep on singing from dusk till dawn.

There are not enough words to describe
The way you'll feel down deep inside
When you really do finally see
The truth in the story about a tree
Falling in the woods with no one around
It would not even make a sound.
That's right, 'cause it takes an ear
Some nerves and brains to make us hear.
It takes an eye to make us see.
Light reflecting off something we call a tree
So if you apply this to all your thoughts
You'll soon realize what is true and false.
Then you too will be ready to say
I'm going to sing a Happy Song today.
I'm going to sing me a Happy Song.
I'm going to sing it on and on.
I don't care what all the others do.
I'm going to sing my Happy Song for you.

I don't really care who you are
You may be a bum or you may be a star.
All that matters is what you think
Cause what you think is what you are.
You can practice peace or you can study war.
You can stand still or you can go far.
All you need to be on your way
Is to sing you a Happy Song today.
What would happen now if I don't think?
Would the World I know start to shrink?
You can study hard and you can study long.

You can get a headache or sing a Happy Song.
I'm going to sing me a Happy Song.
I'm going to sing it loud and strong.
I don't care what comes along.
I'm going to sing a Happy Song.

I don't care who you are trying to impress
With your expensive taste and fancy dress.
Stop and think what we'll all be worth
If we keep on pillaging Mother Earth.
If we stop piling up riches and start learning to share
And begin to treat our planet with tender love and care.
Happiness would soon spread all throughout the land.
Everybody would be wanting to join our happy band.
Maybe someday we may all get along.
We may even learn to know right from wrong.
We are all pretty weak but we could be so strong.
If we would all get together and sing us a Happy Song.
I'm going to sing us a Happy Song.
I'm going to sing it on and on.
I really do care what the others do.
So I'm going to sing my Happy Song for you.

Joy would sometimes overcome me while I was trying to sing and play my *Happy Song*. It isn't an ordinary song but it is to my way of thinking a perfect recipe for happiness. It's a complete list of ingredients like keeping a positive attitude, if you don't like your reality, then change it. The illusions created by our senses, your thoughts make you what you are. Dream or meditate yourself into a world more suitable. If we all could realize that we are all component parts to the same whole thing we could easily create a happy world for everyone overnight. What could be happier than that?

I couldn't hardly wait to get other people's reaction to *Happy Song* and how it all came about which was still a mind-blower to me. A few people didn't want to hear it or about it. Some walked off in the middle of it and some looked at me as if I was crazy. Fortunately some people actually enjoyed it and a few were just as awed by it as I was. The smarter the people were who heard it, the better they liked it. No I am not kidding. I can read most people like a book. I have studied behavior with a passion all my life. You can't bullshit an old bullshitter. I'm not talking about I.Q. or how many degrees you have hanging on your wall. I'm talking about your spiritual awareness, which is the only real measure. Some of the dumbest dummies I know happen to know a lot of stuff, but if you don't know the right stuff, you don't know enough.

Don't worry I'm not going to expose you to anything too dangerous, 'cause if you are not ready to learn, it will fly over your head anyway. I will caution you though, if you are understanding what I've said up till now, I don't have to remind you that this stuff is high voltage and you don't need to play around with it. You know what they say about death, don't you? It is the biggest rush of all and that is why it is saved till last. So don't scare yourself to death when you realize that you are not your body.

I was looking for my old guitar music book so I could name the notes that were the music for *Happy Song*. I still couldn't play it and couldn't tell anyone else how, so I was going to write it down one note at a time. I came across an old note pad that had this written on it. Figure it out. What does it mean? Is it a joke or is it a scheme?

CHAPTER THREE
FIGURE IT OUT

Evidently, this poem had been trying to come in for years because I vaguely remembered writing it down because it had just popped into my mind the way it was written, and I thought at the time that it would make a good song lyric. I remembered at the time thinking about the lady with all those shoes and the new White House dishes. That was how long ago I had written that down. If I had been spiritually aware enough then I would not have had to go through all that pain, but I am not complaining. Those broke feet turned out to be the best thing that ever happened to me, because there is no telling how much more time I would have let my ego cheat me out of experiencing this degree of spiritual energy. I can now understand why those monks go up in the mountains and live in caves for years. I think I would now make a good hermit.

But back to *Figure It Out*. This was perfect and by now I figured I could write songs and this would be just what I needed for the flip-side of *Happy Song*, so I started trying to write *Figure It Out*. I have to take responsibility for most of this poem because I now think it was probably my ego's way of trying to wake up everybody who is so caught up in all the bullshit that permeates the collective ego consciousness. Even my ego wants everyone to be happy whether that is the master plan or not. This poem took a long time to write because it was a product of my ego more than a product of my spirit but I just felt like it had to be written. I wanted to point out how absolutely ridiculous our ego motivated behavior is and how it has affected and permeated our normal human political, social, business and religious world. We have become so accustomed to the insanity that we usually over look it rather than question it.

FIGURE IT OUT

I wonder if the President was telling us a tale
When he said he smoked pot but he didn't inhale.
He seems to me like the kind of a guy
Who will tell the truth ten ways to keep from telling a lie.
Figure It Out.

When another President was a Governor this is what he said,
About the flying saucer that was hovering over his head,
"When I get to Washington, I'll tell you all I've heard and read."
If I told a tale that tall, my face would be permanently red.
Figure It Out.

Another President went to Washington and studied the issues
About the first thing he did was buy the White House new dishes.
Figure It Out and tell me what does it mean.
Is it just a joke or some kind of a scheme?
Is this really real or just a bad dream?
Hope I wake up soon I'm about ready to scream.

The big championship prize-fight redefined fear
It was stopped to keep the chump from eating the champ's ear.
Another champ said, "Fighting is alright if it is done for fun."
They took away his title cause he refused to use a gun.
Figure It Out.

Remember the lady on the news who was crying the blues.
The one who only had several thousand pairs of shoes.
The only thing about it I thought was kind of neat
Was that she only had one pair of feet.
Figure It Out.

Was anybody shocked when the news report said
that the mayor of our National Capitol was a crack-head.
Figure It Out.

The nanny got mandatory life for shaking the baby too hard.
It seemed like it caught the whole world off guard.
When the Judge said, "Nanny everything's gonna be alright.
You've been here long enough;
I'm gonna send you home tonight."
Figure It Out.

When that wacky Iraqi was terrorizing the land.
They let him go without even spanking his hand.
Now it looks like he's going to try it again
And our troops will be back out there wallowing in the sand.
Figure It Out.

That football player's trials, now that was kind of funny.
How one saved his ass and the other took all his money.
Figure It Out and tell me what does it mean?
Is it just a joke or some kind of scheme?
Is it really real or just a bad dream?
Hope I wake up soon I'm about ready to scream.

Some of those preachers I see on TV
Are starting to begin to worry me.
They are going to have to face reality and see
That it is really very hard to take them seriously.
When they say send your money to the Lord but address it to me.
Figure It Out.

How about all those people who are worth a few billion.
I'll bet they won't quit stacking it when it reaches a trillion.

There are a whole lot of folks who don't have a dime.
They have to live on the streets where they're victims of crime.
But look what happened when the Princess died,
Millions and millions of dollars worth of flowers arrived.
Figure It Out.

Are you working all day for a little bit of pay,
Which you will probably just stash or piddle away.
With no time of your own or for friends or home,
Or to get out and roam or just for being alone.
Figure It Out.

I feel real sorry for lots of people I know
Fighting a losing battle with an outrageous ego.
Seems their life is in a rut with only one way to go;
Deeper and deeper into trouble and woe
Between the credit card and the bank account,
Life seems to revolve around the amount
Of money they have and the money they owe.
But, they can't take it with them when it's their time to go.

Figure it out and tell me what does it mean.
Is it just a joke or some kind of a scheme?
Is it really real or just a bad dream?
Hope I wake up soon; I'm about to scream!

The way everybody's talking about the end of time
Seems our chances of survival ain't worth a dime.
Have you tried to overcome all your life's mistakes?
Will the path you're on lead you through the Pearly Gates?
Will you go to Hell and sit there and roast
Or will you hang around here and become a ghost?
Do you think that when you die it will all end,
Or will you have to come back and try it again?
Figure It Out.

If you were born poor or cripple or crazy,
Was it because in another life you were lazy,
Or hateful or greedy, or mean or uncaring,
Or just for judging folks by the clothes they are wearing?
Figure It Out.

Is it something in your soul that makes you crave gold,
Or do you get that way by how you live every day?
Are you loving and kind?
Do you have peace of mind?
Or do you feel like a fighter at the end of his bout
Like him you have a choice just
Figure It Out.

There are so many things we just don't understand.
Can we fix this mess before it is completely out of hand?
Before we are dead why don't we go ahead
And figure out what life is all about
If we are smart then we had better start
Thinking about figuring and *Figure It Out.*
I feel real sure that without a doubt
Somebody somewhere is going to
 Figure It Out.

    I had so much fun analyzing *Sand Bar Saturday Night* that I decided to go back and go over this one with you too. History repeats, they almost caught him with his pants down but this one is a little harder to swallow. Don't smoke any pot before you read this or you might bust a gut—that is if you inhale. At least the peanut man was honest enough to admit lusting over those playboy bunnies. It is too bad that he got lockjaw on the subject matter that is only just the most important information in the whole universe to human kind. You don't suppose that maybe he found out that these clowns are not running the show after all, or maybe he wasn't a clown but his brother is. Just what does it mean? Is there really some intelligence behind it all, and I ain't just talking about the Central Agency kind. What about the old White House dishes? I wonder if they passed them out to all the Washington, D.C. homeless people who were living in cardboard boxes and eating out of garbage cans.

They took the world heavy weight prize fighting championship title away from one of the most respected and loved and deserving Americans of all times because he refused to participate in their dirty little war. Now this other ear-biting, whining crybaby is trying to flash enough money to buy another crack at the title and it looks like he might get it. Am I the one who is crazy for noticing all this stuff?

How many pairs of shoes does it take for the rich and powerful to be happy? Apparently, it is more than several thousand pairs. Washington, D.C. is the headquarters for our only war at the moment. The war on drugs. No wonder its highest city official admits that he is a crackhead. Who was that person who said that we have met the enemy and he is us?

How about this? The nanny who shook the baby was up for murder and convicted to a mandatory life time sentence and the judge sent her home the very same night. What is going on?

Talking about getting away with murder... Apparently if you can hire enough fancy lawyers, you can stack up enough bullshit to be acquitted and miss out on the Death Row experience. Then another court on the same murders decides you are guilty after all and will be satisfied to let you go after taking all your money that the first lawyers failed to get. How can you be guilty and innocent when you are talking about the same crime? I predicted on the day of the car chase that he was guilty, but because he was such a big cog in the giant TV propaganda machine, they had to get him off, and that is exactly what happened. Why else would that detective who had used the N-word on a tape, that was known about by the department, through the wife of the guy who was later named as judge in the trial, sent to the crime scene for a couple of hours in the middle of the night? I ain't Dick Tracy but I can put two and two together.

If one of those Georgia game wardens see you toss even an empty oil can into the river around here, your ass is on the way to Bainbridge. It's a pity that they weren't around when that desert king was dumping enough oil in the Gulf to make a one hundred and fifty mile long oil slick, and setting all those oil wells on fire and killing and looting and waving around all those weapons that were furnished by the same government that finally went to war with him. What a war that was. I watched the whole thing on the news channel. He got out without a scratch. I wonder if that had anything to do with the big meeting in Geneva that was on the news a couple of years earlier where all the oil giants of the world got together to figure out a way to drive oil prices up. They damn sure went up, and he is still talking shit. That war wasn't just good for the oil companies, the military armament business picked up considerably also.

Now what can I say about TV evangelists? They are already headed for self destruction because they are their own worst enemy. I would sure hate to be in their shoes when Jesus does show up. Go ahead and send them your money; you are probably going to just throw it away anyway. That is unless you are one of those tight bastards who thinks that if they can stack it a little bit higher, they might find security and respect from the poor people scratching out a living on the street. Then when they die everybody will make a fuss over them and send acres of flowers to their funeral like they did to the Princess. I don't think her money is what motivated their attention. She knew that there was nothing royal about royalty.

I'm so close to living on the street myself, I have huge respect for the poor people who can maintain without all the trappings of money and material things and still be satisfied to have plenty of time for themselves.

The people I feel sorry for are just about everybody I know. No matter how much money and things they have, it is not near enough now and it is so easy to buy stuff on time and credit that you can become a slave real quick, and you ain't a whole lot of fun no more. Even as powerful as those Egyptian Pharaohs were, all that gold and treasures they tried to take with them, was found thousands of years later collecting dust. All you leave this planet with, unless you are an astronaut, is spiritual awareness, and if you haven't got some stashed somewhere, then the joke is on you, and if you can't wake up out of a bad dream, then you really are going to have something to worry about.

We may not have much time left at the rate we are going. What if there is something to all those prophecies out there, warning of major Earth changes and mass destruction? Are you ready to shove off tonight? You won't have to pack, 'cause you are going like you are. Tonight might be your night. What if you knew that it was going to be tomorrow night? What changes would you try to make or have you been trying to make them all along? Suppose that you didn't get around to making them? Are you good enough at making excuses that you will get by? Don't count on it. There are some people who have apparently been so attached to this world and its material things that they still can't break its hold on them and their spirit has lingered around as a ghost for sometimes hundreds of years after the body dies. Talk about a bad dream! All of those ghost stories have the same agenda.

If you don't believe in reincarnation, you need to do your homework, because you don't know anything about it. There are tons of documented evidence to support it and nothing makes more sense than that spiritually speaking. It explains everything from what is your situation on Earth to why it is that way. Who were those wise men who showed up from the Orient, and how did they arrive just in time with gifts for the birth that took place on the road in a manger? Did they trace out an expected incarnation as they are still doing today? What about the star that led them? If it happened today would it have been called a UFO? We have telescopes today that can see as far as you can see and they haven't found that star yet. They haven't found any UFOs either if you rely on what your leaders tell you. They told us that Russians were coming to get us for thirty years until all of a sudden one morning they said there was no longer a Russia. Now, we are buddies and we have started sending our astronauts to their space station.

A few months ago, the press blasted us with news that they found a very large asteroid on collision course with the Earth due to slam into us in about thirty years. The very next day, all those reporters said not to worry because NASA came up with some new figures that said that it was going to miss us after all. The very biggest news story of the millennium completely reversed in one day. Imagine that! I don't think they were lying about the asteroid, but I'm not too sure which set of numbers were correct. There are enough asteroids between the solid planets and the gaseous ones to build a planet the size of our moon. It ain't if we are going to get hit, but when will it happen? Government policy already states that in case of an event of that magnitude, they would not even warn the masses of people until the last thing because it would create too much confusion. Imagine that! Remember how they almost burned down Los Angeles when the tapes of those cops beating that black man showed up on the news. I wouldn't want to have to tell everybody that the world is about to explode and we don't have quite enough space stations or underground shelters that we built with your money without asking your permission to accommodate everyone either. Wasn't there something in history about "...of the people, by the people, for the people and created equal, and pursuit of happiness and liberty and justice for all...," and the cow jumped over the moon!

Maybe the ancient sorcerers were correct in believing that human emotions are being cultivated for food by the inorganic beings cause it looks like they are having a bumper crop. Where could we even start to fix this mess we're in? I don't think humans

39

are going to do it alone in this lifetime. Maybe I am crazy to think that it is all messed up in the first place. It sure ain't the way I would do it, but I can't even comprehend total awareness. I would have probably bitched about dinosaurs too.

Scientists have located the crater of the asteroid strike that killed off all the dinosaurs at one time sixty-five million years ago. Evidence indicates that they were part of the planet for millions of years and all vanished over night. Where does that fit into the story of creation? Which day did that happen? Creation is an ongoing process that has continued since it started until today. Evolutionists have determined that a bantam rooster is T-Rex's cousin.

Is it going to take another asteroid strike or something of that magnitude to get people to wake up and take their heads out of their ass and stop swallowing all the bullshit and to learn something about taking responsibility for their actions? How did that preacher get nine hundred people to drink poisoned Kool-Aid? Why would anyone take a bomb to the Olympic Games? Has business greed caused some people to feel justified when they rob a store with a mask and gun instead of being robbed by the store which doesn't even need a mask or gun? Is your professional license just a license to steal? Does it really entitle you to charge ten or a hundred times as much to a customer as you would pay someone who does an equal amount of real work, like hauling off your garbage or cleaning your house or growing your food? Is a single C.E.O. or movie star or singer or athlete worth more for a few months than a hundred school teachers or health care workers for a whole year? How can you become a millionaire or billionaire without taking advantage of other poor people caught up in your wheeling and dealing? Just how many times can you mark up your goods or services and maintain love for your neighbor as you love yourself? Churches are full of people and are even created by people who don't understand that you cannot worship two masters. Organized religion is a business. They handle an enormous pile of money, and money is the barometer that measures ego. Your ego is what keeps you out of tune with spirit and if you spend your energy feeding money to the ego then you are robbing your spirit with every cent you accumulate. Survival dictates that we all use money, but when you find someone whose life revolves around it, you better keep both eyes on them if you have to have any association with them. Ask any businessman or TV evangelist or crook or drug dealer or hit man or pimp or prostitute or burglar or politician what led them to do such horrible and uncaring things to themselves and others and if they don't lie about it the answer is always summed up with one word -- money, which always equates to power in the material world. The urge to dictate your will over others is really the destructive element that will allow you to build up enough negative karma that you may never get back to the light, like some of those ghosts who have been hanging around for years.

You may say, "But I don't believe in ghosts or psychic phenomena, like ESP or telepathy or clairvoyance or out-of-the-body experiences, or regressive hypnosis or reincarnation or UFO's or astrology or such. I have personally experienced most of those things so I have to believe them. No matter what you have been conditioned to believe or not believe, the truth is always the truth. Every human on this planet that can move his or her arms and legs can swim whether they know it or not, but if they don't believe they can swim, they will probably drown. Same thing with everything else. You will probably never have a spiritual or psychic experience if you don't believe it is possible.

One day I saw on TV that the biography program was going to do a piece on the sleeping prophet who did readings in trance on patients of doctors who had usually given up on them, and not only diagnosed them, but usually told them how to be cured. He did this over several years and for thousands of people successfully even though he had never been trained in the medical field. His work is undisputed and has been accepted as legitimate by everyone who ever investigated him and his ability to know things outside of his normal perception.

I wanted to inform my friend of this so I looked up the number of her parents, who she was visiting with one hundred and fifty miles away. I dialed the number and got a recorded message from the phone company that there was no such number in service. I figured that I must have dialed it wrong so I dialed it again. Again, I got the message that the number was no good. I found out later that the area code had changed. I don't like phones anyway and was annoyed that I couldn't make contact. For some reason I stated her name in a normal voice and asked her to call me. About thirty seconds later, the phone rang, and it was her. The first thing she said was, "Were you trying to get up with me?" I said yes and asked why she had decided to call me at that precise moment. She said that she had been reading a new book about the world's leading psychic authority and the idea to call me just popped into her mind. That rules out coincidence because I not only got her attention but she also got the message. No doubt it happened since we were both tuned in to spiritual consciousness about a spiritual matter. Two days ago while I was working on this part of this book, I went in to get a drink. On the way back, I sat down by the phone and was looking up my daughter's long distance number when the phone rang. It was her Mother calling to tell me that she had just gotten off the phone with our daughter and she wanted me to call her because her son was going to have surgery the next week. I have been on both the sending and receiving end of telepathy so don't try to tell me there is nothing to it. If you invest in Ma-Bell, you may get a wrong number but if you invest in spirit, you can get through when material things crap out. The knowing that I can still communicate with them no matter what happens in the material world is worth more to me than all the gold you could stack up. You can't put a price on the security that, that knowing is worth. You cannot help but feel happy and secure and peaceful and wonderful and thankful when you get a direct shot of spiritual energy like that and you know for sure that you are on the right path.

Now consider an ego motivated energy contact and how you feel about that. A good example of that might be a common human endeavor such as cheating on your taxes. If you have been fair and honest you will approach an audit with the ease of any other daily encounter, but if you have been unfair and cheated, you are going to be stressed no matter how good you are at hiding it. It's the rule of the jungle. If you can't do the time, don't do the crime. You don't see many happy convicts, because not many of them are stupid enough to do the crime if they think they are going to be caught. If you can afford enough lawyers you can get away with about anything at least temporarily. Don't forget though, that for every action, there is an equal and opposite reaction and that is where eye for an eye comes into play. That doesn't mean that if I take your eye that you have the right to take my eye. Not at all, it means that if you take my eye, then before the scales are even, you must have an eye taken from you even if you have to come back again and again until the debt is paid. Therefore, the proper definition of sin is any transgression of selfishness that takes away from the whole or any of its parts. That covers a whole lot more than just the little list that Moses brought down from the mountain.

Electricity only flows while there is a difference of potential between the positive and negative poles, so if your ego has been building up a bunch of negative baggage and if you don't have at least as much positive stacked somewhere, sparks are going to fly. It is just that simple. You might have to stand in line for a long, long time, next time, for even a decrepit body if something drastic happened to the human population, leaving only a few survivors. Think about that.

Don't forget about the thousands of asteroids and comets that are crossing Earth's orbit on a regular basis. We just went through the tail of a comet the other night causing a spectacular light show with particles burning up in our atmosphere. Most of those particles were only dust size. What if they had been a little larger? What about the comet that broke up and hit Jupiter in about two dozen places? Just one of those pieces created a storm the size of the Earth that lasted more than a year. During an announced meteor shower a couple of years ago, I counted fourteen shooting stars in less than an hour that were so large it took over ninety degrees of arc in the sky for them to burn up.

As I'm writing this we have aircraft bombing weapon sites that are thought to contain biological and chemical weapons of mass destruction. How long is it going to be before these are going to be sent back to us? Should I even mention that we have enough nuclear weapons to blow the whole planet into a new asteroid belt and the commander in chief, a proven liar, is about to get shit-canned because he can't keep his pecker in his pants. Then there is an El Niño and global warming and Ebola and fault lines and volcanoes and Earthquakes and acid rain and air and water pollution and toxic waste and computer virus and terrorists and more subtle things less noticeable like huge ice caps at the poles of a spinning mass called Earth, made of trillions and trillions of tons of water removed from the atmosphere and deposited as snow and ice at the most critical position possible to cause precession or slip of the vertical spin axis, by more than twenty degrees, which is about one thousand miles from the magnetic poles where it started. It doesn't take a scientist to determine that something might happen. Any kid who has ever spun a top can tell you what happens when that top leans over and starts wobbling. When gravity overcomes centrifugal force, the top flips over. Geologists say they have evidence that this has happened numerous times and prior north and south poles are dotted all over the globe. This precession is accumulative and is growing every day-night cycle, so you could be sitting on top of a slow ticking time bomb wondering if the market is up or down or if you have purchased enough insurance to be secure, or figuring out something else more drastic to worry about, or you can sing yourself a happy song, if you can.

Let me go back and explain what I said earlier about your spiritual growth depending on the amount of energy you invest into it. I was talking to a friend one day about how it seems that sooner or later just about everybody's ego drags them on a downward spiral until they hit bottom and wallow around in it a while before they find the Lord or wake up to the reality of what a mess their ego has made of their life. Most of us who have experienced this with no other way to go but up, couldn't stop falling and have to make some positive changes or die. The more we change and take responsibility for our condition the more we start to feeling better and acting better and being better and this snowball effect grows with leaps and bounds. Now if you don't realize that it is your spirit that is affecting the outcome, by the amount of energy that ego used to waste but is now invested into spirit, then you just might identify the Lord as what did it, and you might start worshiping some religious figure and there are a heap of them and none of them wanted to be worshiped any way. If you think that God was powerful enough to create the universe, then he was certainly not insecure enough to need humans to worship Him. If you change the focus of your energy toward spirit, you can get the same result by worshiping a pumpkin because that religious figure of your choice would inform you that he or she and the pumpkin were equals since they were both going to die and return to spiritual oneness. So beware, you could get so busy hunting God out there that you might miss seeing Him inside yourself.

But anyway, I figured out why you can fall so fast and why you can climb back up so fast, and it is very easy to understand. I'll explain it to you.

Imagine a ruler and let one end of it represent total maximum ego. The other end will represent total maximum spirit. So half way or six inches represents one half ego and one half spirit, and for simplicity, let's say that six is where you are located right now in your evolutionary journey back to spirit where it all began. Ego was created at birth when you were all spirit. That accounts for a baby's ability to learn so rapidly. Ego has not developed enough for a few years to get in the way.

My grandson, a normal child could perform about a dozen physical exercises on verbal command at the age of one, like waving hello or goodbye or spitting out his pacifier, or giving you five or clapping his hands. He would even fake a cough over and over if he got some attention every time he did it. Just think that from two cells and one year and nine months to all this.

Look at the ruler in Figure 1 below and by comparing your honest feelings to those on the stick. You can get a rough idea of what ratio of ego to spirit you are.

Max Ego

Inches	Figure 1	Figure 2	Figure 3	Figure 4	Figure 5	Figure 6
1	Despair	Millions of			End Here	
2	Hate	Dollars				
3	Fear					Invest 3
4	Worry	Thousands of				
5	Sadness	Dollars	Invest 1 in.		Invest	
6	Satisfied		Start Here	Start Here	Start Here	Start/End Here
7	Successful	Hundreds of	End Here	Invest 6		
8	Joyous	Dollars				
9	Caring					Invest 3
10	Peaceful	Tens of				
11	Happy	Dollars				
12	Ecstasy			End Here		

Max Spirit

In Figure 2, you can fill in your own amount of dollars or hundreds, or thousands, or millions of dollars that you want the twelve to represent. If you only require twelve dollars to maintain, you are already a saint and you should be writing this book. If you are in the twelve hundred dollar range, you are probably smiling. If you are in the twelve thousand dollar range, look out! If you are in the twelve million dollar range, you had better call Doctor Kevorkian before you really get yourself in a jam.

But for this example in Figure 3 though, let's just use inches of energy for simplicity and that you are half way back to spirit at six inches   Ego has taken its toll on all of us over the life times or trips through the physical plane or whatever you want to call it. All energy spent accumulating money and material possessions moves you toward the ego-end of the ruler which craves those things. All the energy spent giving away excess money and material things by doing unto others and loving thy neighbor as thyself moves you toward the spirit-end of the ruler where those things are neither wanted nor needed.

So, here you sit at six on the scale and let's say that fate has provided you with all you need plus another person's equal share, which totals up to your three plus another three for a sum total of six shares of energy so that you can afford to share. If you decide to use one inch worth of that extra energy on yourself rather than use it on someone else, then you move to five, and later you decide that maybe you should have invested it into spirit instead, it will take another inch worth of your stack just to get back to your starting point at six. Then, it will cost you yet another inch to move to seven. So if you make the wrong choice it will take three inches worth of energy to achieve the same goal that the right choice only took one inch to achieve. Get the picture? Eventually, you will finally realize that all energy above what you really, really need that is invested into ego is ultimately wasted because the energy consumed by ego is lost at the death of the body and all that is left to spend eternity with is that which was invested in spirit.

So again in Figure 4, remember we have all we need which is three and another three to invest. Suppose we invest all six inches worth of our extra toward spirit. We will then end up at maximum spirit or twelve inches and will still have all we need.

Now in Figure 5, suppose we invest all six inches of our extra to ego. We end up at zero or maximum ego, but at least we still have all we need but it will take all that just to get back to starting point six if we decide to go back and you will soon want to go back because you will find out that some nasty characters hang out at that end of the stick.

Now let's suppose that we're at six with six more to invest as in Figure 6. We decide to invest three inches to ego and three inches to spirit. Guess what? We are still at six and the three inches we invested toward spirit were canceled out by the three inches spent on ego so that spirit's three inches didn't even count. Scary ain't it?

What that means is that if you are not investing at least fifty-one percent of your energy toward spirit, you are losing ground this time around. Your church is letting you off easy with just a ten percent tithe so you had better have some real charity contributions to go along with it or you might be in a heap of trouble. Here's more bad news. Don't get caught in the trap of claiming all your friends and relatives that you have aided because they have to be placed in the ego column because they are important to your ego or they would probably have received the same that the strangers got, if anything. Good luck!

Be careful how you invest your energy because your spirit is going to be around a whole lot longer than your ego. In fact, it will wear out numerous egos before it gains enough energy to be free to come and go in this vibratory frequency at will.

Even though my ego might want to see everybody happy, my spirit knows that most of us, as victims of a shooting or stabbing or rape or robbery or murder or about anything else, are just experiencing the consequences of a previous similar behavior on our part from this life or one a million years ago. That doesn't mean that you can't be happy though. You can't help but be happy when you have spiritual energy flowing through you. The choice is yours. You may be surprised to find out that there are many, many unhappy millionaires who are totally miserable.

I have found that throughout my personal life my happiest periods coincided with my periods of least wealth and my most unhappy times came during my most prosperous times. Figure that out! Now you have been notified and my responsibility ends here. Now yours begins.

By the way, that ruler doesn't just work on money, it also measures compassion and caring and love and how you treat others. Common sense tells you that it is easy to love someone nice, but it is hard to love an asshole, although that is where you build up energy inches.

Our spirit and ego consciousness is so intertwined that it is hard to separate them precisely or tell which is which. If you prayed all day that could be spiritual if you prayed for everybody; otherwise, it could be worthless if presented as a shopping list.

Everything on this planet is a component part of Earth very much like every nut and bolt and tube and diode and switch and wire and knob on your TV set is a part of it. If you alter any of the parts on that TV in anyway, you could lose your picture for good. Just open up the back of a TV set in view of anyone who has never seen a TV turned on, if there are any left on Earth, and ask them to guess what this box full of stuff is and what it does. Not a single one of them would even come close to imagining the magic of television.

We are just as naive about our Earth and solar system. What is a Monarch butterfly's role in returning every year at the same time to the same few acres, by the billions, after traveling thousands of miles in all directions? What about the swallows in San Juan Capistrano, or a salmon returning from thousands of miles across deep oceans to the exact spot in the stream where it was born, or lobsters lining up in single file for miles and crawling across the ocean floor. Why are the distances between and the size of the Earth, moon, and sun just exactly precise to allow both a total lunar and solar eclipse?

Humans don't even know what humans are, much less butterflies or lobsters or swallows or salmon. Human egos see everything as either commodities or as useless objects if they can't think of any way to exploit them. We are already on the verge of losing our picture for good and conditions are getting worse each day, and here I am just beginning to love this marvelous miraculous world and enjoy fully every second I am here. Wouldn't you care to do the same? You know who the villain is? I would love to pick up all those people and shake the shit out of them till they come to their senses, but I would have to shake damn near everybody on Earth. Look what is going on.

Try to forget for a few minutes your individuality as a human and think of yourself as you really are, a component part of planet Earth. How have you treated the rest of Earth's components and how do you feel about that? Humans are capable of destroying not just the parts but the whole thing including himself. Among the humans who are supposedly running the show, government officials, business executives, college administrators, scientists, religious leaders, lawyers, bankers, insurance men and other assorted assholes are some of the most unethical humans you will find. Work has already begun to completely change the whole environment on Mars so that humans will have some place to go when they totally screw up Earth, and the moon will become a loading dock. No wonder we have been kept in the isolation ward of the universe, but there is a pass key. If you can maintain the perspective of doing your best as a part of it all and adopt the attitude that all of it is part of you and if you treat every part of it the way you treat yourself, then God will smile on you. Then you might see why it is obscene to spend three million dollars for a famous baseball or to buy any amount of the human bullshit. Our forefathers have inhabited Earth in some human form for millions of years, barely leaving a trace. How do you feel about the impact you have made on Mother Earth? How does she feel about it? Is she going to save you for seed or plow you under? You might better think about that.

I think, I think I am; therefore, I am, I think. In the beginning man created himself. Then he created the world and all its inhabitants. Then he created God in his own image. I tell every religious fanatic I talk with, that you cannot study enough religious philosophies to find the truth if they contradict the idea that man created God. Only from that point of view are you able to digest the information that supports that truth. Consider these facts.

All isolated people all over the planet and as far back as we can trace, have known that there is more to us than just the physical part; therefore, most of them have attributed this to a supernatural power called God. This God has many, many first names and all subscribers to this attitude believe that my God can beat up your God, so that now God has taken on the ego's attributes of all the descriptions or discussions about Him. Very sophisticated ways of behavior have been fashioned to worship Him and enforce His laws which really are actually man's laws attributed to God.

Fact number two: Each human being is more than just the body and takes up considerably more space on the energy spectrum than the small bands represented by the margins of the physical senses through which the body perceives the whole universal energy. We also have access to extra sensory perception, if we are able to tune into those other frequencies which are in the range where God resides, and when noticed, are termed "miracles." So if you can tune them in then they become a part of you.

Fact number three: Humans learn from birth to recognize various energy patterns and to identify them as components of the world thus creating the world in their mind through a filter of sensory perception. So we all see light reflecting off some energy mass that looks like what we have previously identified as a mallard duck and if it feels and smells and sounds and tastes like a duck, then our brain prints out duck and that is that. Our brain-sensory system is constantly scanning energy through this human being filter and is thus creating a totally different world than the one the duck is creating through its sensory perception system.

So because of all the various ways of perceiving this ball of energy we all call Earth, then we must understand that our so called world only exists at that particular frequency of human sensory perception and does not exist to the mallard, even though he inhabits the very same ball of energy, but it won't look or be the same to him. That is what I mean when I say that we create ourselves and our world. If you can broaden your spectrum of perception to include some other sensory perception that is lying dormant at the fringes of consciousness waiting for your ego to O.D., then you can create your own world, by including the higher senses, on a larger scale than most folks can even imagine.

Fact number four: Human beings spend more or less one third of their entire time on Earth with the body asleep, thus leaving the higher consciousness, that is not directly involved with the physical, free to roam about unfettered by time or space because they only exist in the physical world, so we are free to visit other realities that we know as dreams. We all dream a lot every night although most of us forget them almost immediately upon waking, because our ego consciousness, that most of us inhabit almost exclusively, doesn't speak the language and wasn't even present during the dream. So ego usually explains them away as fantasies or unreal memories conjured up by our thoughts and mind. That place you dreamed about last night that you now don't have a clue to its location, was created by you the same way you created the "real world" that you are in now. Furthermore, where did the "real world" go while you were in the dream world? They were both in the same place in your mind but were of a different frequency because they were perceived by two different sets of sensory preceptors. It becomes apparent then that our view of a solid, rather than a thought world is only located at the point of our attention, which is our tuning knob. It is almost like being able to watch football or boxing or a fishing show on the same TV at the same time just by varying the frequency by changing the channel.

Fact number five: In the millions of years man has lived on Earth he has not been able to produce even one piece of evidence toward the existence of God. You cannot use the old, just look around at what all he created, thing when you wake up and realize that everything is still in the process of creation. Which came first, the chicken or the egg? Did Adam have a belly button? You can't step into the same river twice because you will be stepping into new water every time.

Everything in the whole universe above the temperature of absolute zero, is and has always been in a constant state of change and the only place in the whole universe where absolute zero is found so far is on a chalkboard in some university physics lab.

We are finding out that humans and apes are even closer cousins than even the evolutionists suspected. Over ninety-eight and four-tenths percent of our DNA blueprint is identical and chimpanzees are now being taught sign language and communicating complicated information with their keepers. What are they going to say about zoos?

Scientists have catalogued and studied in every way that you can, millions of species of life on Earth from plants and animals and birds and insects and fish and bacteria and viruses and everything you can think of. They have even started naming the stars, but you know what, there is not a single entry under God, devil either.

Why am I going to so much trouble trying to explain something so simple? We come into this world with so much potential but due to our stars and karma or God's plan, we have to wade through mountains of conditioned bullshit just so that we can inherit mountains of knowledge when we sift through it all.

It is already Y2K and some people's understanding of the human condition is still pre-stone age. Look in the mirror and ask yourself, "Am I really as dumb as this bastard thinks I am?" If the answer is yes, there may be some hope for you after all.

If your answer is No, then maybe you will explain to me why you get up every morning and go off to work all day in some awful place doing some aggravating chore that requires your complete attention, just so that you can buy a bunch of pretty shiny junk that you don't need to go along with all that other junk you already have, so that you don't have to cower down to your neighbor who has more junk than you. Then every April, you send Uncle Sam a huge chunk of change so that he can buy more and better war equipment so that he can further and further intimidate you to give him more and more and allow him to make more and more music for you to dance to and to tell you every move to make and now he has the capability to see that you do it too. A recent movie line about some Russians defecting to the USA was, "When I get to America, I want to travel around and see all the states I can. Do you have to have papers to travel there?" The reply was, "No, no papers." Bullshit! First off, if you are going to stay legal and not break any laws and if you are going to have to do any work, then you must have a social security card. If you don't look or sound like the folks around here, you will need a green card or your immigration papers and if you work for yourself, you will need permits and license, proof of workman's compensation, liability insurance and letters of recommendation. Then if you drive a vehicle to get around, you will need a driver's license and your vehicle will need a registration and proof of insurance. So unless you are already independently wealthy enough that you don't have to or want to hunt or fish for food, will also need a hunting license with a deer stamp and migratory bird stamp and a duck stamp or trapping permit. Then, if you hunt or fish out of a boat, it will need registration papers. If you fish in saltwater, you will need a saltwater fishing license, and if you fish in freshwater, you will need a freshwater license. If you want to use more than twenty-five hooks on your trotline, you will need a commercial license, and if you want to dip up some crawfish for bait out of a road side ditch, you will also need a crawfish stamp. If you are lucky or should I say unlucky enough to talk your main squeeze into bedding down, you will also need a marriage license. It would take an awfully big pine tree to make enough paper to print all that bullshit on, and a briefcase to tote it all in.

But don't get caught without any of it, cause if you are not a good ole boy or know somebody well who is, you could be in a heap of trouble. If you can't pay all those fines, you might find yourself rooming with the real criminals. Yes, the murderers and rapists and robbers of all kinds and possessors of controlled substances.

Uncle Sam, or is it Big Brother now, whatever doesn't care if you drink alcohol or coffee, which are some of the most addictive substances you can find, till it is coming out of your ears or if you smoke a dozen packs of taxed cigarettes a day even though they admit and even warn you on the package about the hazards to your health. But don't get caught possessing even one joint even if you don't even smoke it or inhale, because they haven't figured out a way to tax it and can still make more money on it themselves through fines and confiscation of property and Lord knows what else.

But if you happen to get sick enough and they know for sure that you are going to go blind or die, they will let your doctor give you a little bit for medicine. Look what happened at Woodstock. All those crazy hippies loving one another and protesting war and the destruction of Mother Earth and not a single one of them was wearing a coat and tie, the uniform of the ego. Some of them were even skinny dipping and there was not even one report of negative behavior from a half million stoned people grooving in the rain and mud for three days. No wonder there is a war on drugs and mind-altering substances and plants. If people expand their mind beyond self-consciousness, the brain washing dissolves and then how long will it take before our government self-destructs? Who in the hell is going to go to work or war?

In the sixties, the pot-smokers came out of the closet, and now I know more people who do, or would smoke it, if it were not illegal, than I know who do not or would not. And, I am talking about people who are in all kinds of professions which I am sure Uncle Sam would rather I did not mention. I, myself, have been on some jobs that were so bad and miserable that if you complain about the drugs on the job, you are the one who is shipped out. There are many ways to beat a drug test or drug search, but that is just one more way Big Brother erodes away our civil rights or so-called freedom.

If you stacked up all the law books in one pile, you would no longer need a space shuttle to achieve Earth's orbit. Crime Stoppers, which has not stopped crime, sounds like a good idea, but it was the final nail in our coffin. Now, the Police can legally kick down your door from just one anonymous phone call. So if you want your door kicked down, beat the rush and just write your government a letter because you can't get them on the phone if you have a complaint, and tell them you don't like the way they are running things. They will be glad to kick it down for you.

It is a good thing that those Egyptian Pharaohs didn't come back to life because scientists who were studying their mummies have found out through sophisticated analysis that they had been smoking dope and inhaling it to boot. FDLE would bust them at the border and take away all that gold that they might have left.

If your answer is still "No, I am not crazy," then how are you or your religion going to explain away religious wars? They have only been going on for as far back as what history of humans cover. We are on the brink of world destruction right now due to religious prejudice over who owns what land. Think about the land that you may own right now. Who owned it first and what happened to them? I found a fluted Clovis spear point less than one-half of a mile from the little farm I bought years ago when I still believed that you can own land. Archeologists have dated similar points of that particular style and degree of precision and skill to between ten and twelve thousand years ago around here. It is obvious that this place has been inhabited continuously ever since then because of the climate, beauty, abundance of game and freshwater springs all over the place, and burial and ceremonial mounds and caves and rivers leading to the Gulf.

A famous American Indian chief once made a plea for his people to the American government stating that we cannot sell this land because we do not own this land. This land is our Mother. That means to me that the first owner of any land on this Earth was a thief who stole it from everybody else. So now if your fortune comes from real estate, then you are capitalizing on an unjust deed done in the past and you must assume the responsibility for that action because it too will weigh on your karma scale. Even if you inherited it, you are not morally entitled to it.

Our constitution says that all men are created equal even though some of the men who wrote and signed it, owned slaves at the time. Imagine someone who is important enough to actually own other people. I guess that is a little better than just killing them off and after stealing their land, packing the rest of them off to some desolate reservation.

So no matter how many legal documents you produce, you are still on stolen property. You are going to own a small spot of it someday though, when what you thought was you dies and starts breaking back down into the various elements that formed your body, and becomes fertilizer to support another life of some kind. Some of you will make real good fertilizer because you are already almost pure bullshit.

If your living or fortune came from exploiting Mother Earth, then you are holding on to tainted money. Nothing good ever came from bad seed. Have you ever heard of the curse of the Hope diamond? It is the most precious stone ever mined and was so expensive, it was originally owned only by kings and multimillionaires, and it seemed to bring nothing but bad luck to its long list of owners. I don't think the diamond was the curse, but what it represented which is grand prize in the ego contest. Ego is king of pain and suffering, so if you are waiting on the Lord to come and relieve you of your pain and suffering, your luggage had better not include much more than you actually need to survive as long as there are poor and oppressed people starving on this planet.

He may want to know why you love yourself more than your neighbor or why you got lock-jaw when you should have been speaking out, and why you continually invested in negative behavior rather than trying to leave a positive mark on the world? How is that going to stack up to saying Grace three times a day and going to church a couple of hours a week?

Now if you still think you are sane and I am without doubt, crazy as hell, you may as well go ahead and pick out the most aggravating person you know and give, no sell him this book for Christmas, and waste some of his time too. Best wishes and good luck. You are going to need it.

We are fixing to get to the heavy ammo anyway and you really will think I am nuts. But first, I have just got to tell you about a couple of poems I did just for fun. Along about this place in the story, I had just gotten finished with *Figure It Out* and it was just an assortment of small thoughts that had come in, and I like to have never arranged them in some kind of order.

CHAPTER FOUR
SANDBAR SATURDAY NIGHT

I had been talking to my brother one day and he was telling me about the latest escapades of one of his buddy's "love em and leave em" lifestyle. When he said that BoBo was *talkin' walkin'* again, I said, "That sounds like a country music song title." I got busy trying to write such a song but could just not get anything on the paper but pure junk. Two or three days later, without any luck at all on it, I just happened to wake up one morning singing it and wrote the whole thing before I got out of bed. It was all new material and I had even made a mistake by one word, thus changing the theme of the whole thing, because I was writing it down so fast so I wouldn't forget it. My musical buddy pointed out my error and was able to supply the two lines I just couldn't seem to find to complete it. A one and a two and *talkin' walkin'*.

TALKIN' WALKIN'

I walked into the bar one day
Just in time to hear BoBo say
When it comes to breaking camp
You could say that I'm the champ!
If she starts giving me crap,
I'll grab my coat and put on my cap!
I'll go to the truck and get out my map
And I'll start planning me a walkabout.
I'm talking walking, and I ain't balking,
I'll let my feet do all my talking
I ain't going to listen to no damn squawking!
Read my lips - I'm talking walking!

59

If she starts fussing and she won't quit,
It won't even worry me a little bit.
No, I won't pitch me a royal fit
I'll just pack my sack and git.
He said if she starts to showing her tail
I'll start packing instead of raising hell.
Since I know that I can't make bail
I'll take off before I land in jail.
I'm talking walking, and I ain't balking
I'll let my feet do all my talking
I ain't going to listen to no damn squawking
Read my lips – I'm talking walking!

Well, I hadn't seen BoBo since I don't know when
But when I did, I asked him where he had been.
He looked down with a sheepish grin and said,
"I moved out. But I moved back in.
I took her to the beach. We were gonna try it again.
I'm tired of walking. This time, I'm balking.
My feet quit talking and I enjoy squawking.
Read my lips – I'm tired of talking. Goodbye.

A short while later when my brother was working nearby, we decided to set out a couple of short trotlines. I had just gotten to where I could barely get around on crutches. It was like going to heaven to be out on that river again! I could almost throw a rock the distance I was staying from a huge lake, formed by a dammed up river 14 miles downstream. I fell off the bank about 25 miles below the dam, and hadn't seen any water since, outside of the bathtub. Conditions were just right and fish were biting good. We were joking around about writing a song about catfishing. He said something like having a fight on Saturday night at a sandbar. My mind turned into a poem factory and my thoughts started coming out in rhymes, and I was so excited I could hardly wait to get back to the house so I could start writing. This was a subject that I knew something about, and I was going to write this poem! I worked on it most of that night and all day long the next few days, and named it *Sandbar Saturday Night*.

SANDBAR SATURDAY NIGHT

Catfishing is more than a hobby of mine,
I'm ready to go about any time.
Hot or cold, rain or shine,
Day or night, I don't mind!
I like to set bush hooks or run a trotline,
A cypress slat basket suits me just fine.
But when I really want to get me a thrill,
A rush so big it makes me squeal!,
Words can't describe the way I feel
When I hook into a big one on a rod and reel!
Fishing is hard sometimes, almost seems like work.
But that all disappears with just one little jerk.
Best time I ever had was one Saturday night
Down at the sandbar, trying to pick a fight.
I had two rods out, both set just right.
West wind was blowing, not a cloud in sight.
Millions of stars were twinkling bright,
Red and blue and silver and white!
I was munching on cheese curls and sipping on Sprite,
I checked the water level again, the rise was very slight.
I'd been there about an hour and hadn't had a single bite!
I was trying to sit still and trying to be quiet.
Had the lantern turned down, didn't want too much light,
My bait cup was smelling a little past real ripe!
When all of a sudden my line jerked tight.
He swallowed my bait on his very first strike.

Felt the hook stick in and experienced momentary fright,
Survival glands kicked in and it was fight or flight.
He took off with both, with all his might.
My rod exploded into motion like dynamite!
The tip is under the boat, completely out of sight,
All I could do was hang on real tight.
I finally reached the lantern and turned up the light,
I had a brand new line and the drag was working right.
I knew I was going to have some fun tonight!
He ran up the river, turned left, then right
Back down river again, stretching my line real tight.
Again and again he repeated this rite
Then he came by the boat, and there in the light
We were eye to eye. What a magnificent sight!
I wonder what he thought, seeing what I looked like?
We were aye to aye, both the captain of our life,
Both have had our share of trouble and strife,
Each toting his own type of razor sharp knife.
His around his neck, and mine strapped to my thigh.
We were I to I in an ego's fight.
We were both out cruising, late at night,
Looking for some action, checking every site.
Thinking everything is gonna be alright,
If he'd been paying attention with his senses just right,
He would have noticed my hook, cause it was big and bright.
He wouldn't be in trouble, if he'd kept his mouth shut tight.
He was out hunting food, then fighting for his life.
But the Lord will decide who will win tonight.
If he gets away, okay, it will be alright.
If he doesn't, I'm going to eat some catfish with delight!
Of course, there is no guarantee that I'll survive this fight,
My heart is pounding, my knuckles are white,
I'm gasping for breath and my chest feels tight.
My blood pressure is up, cholesterols are out of sight!

While checking my pulse I hummed "I saw the light,"
I wonder if this is what heaven is like?
I didn't realize my knees were so weak,
Till my butt made contact with that cold, boat seat!
The fight was nearly over and I got him in my net,
But he didn't quit splashing till I was soaking wet!
I've been looking for something, but I haven't found it yet.
That is anywhere close to the excitement that I get,
Dipping 20 pounds of catfish with a ten pound net,
Some people don't cat fish, they have too much class,
It drives them crazy when my bait is the size of a trophy bass!
It may sound strange, but it is a natural fact,
It takes twice as long to get there as it does to get back!
Got enough fish here to last all week,
Snatched off his hide and cut him up real neat,
Fired off the cooker and turned up the heat,
My taste buds were ready for a special treat.
Fixed myself a drink and got ready to eat.
A fresh-fried strip of catfish meat
With cheese grits and hushpuppies, that is hard to beat.
After another plate or two and something sweet,
I kicked back in my chair and propped up my feet,
In about five minutes I was sound asleep!
Dreaming about a river that was clean, clear, and deep
With a nice sandy bank that's not too steep,
Right below the mouth of a pretty little creek.
The wild flowers were beautiful and they smelled so sweet,
An ice chest full of goodies was serving as my seat.
There was a natural pole-holder that was absolutely neat,
Formed by a little stump right between my feet.
I dipped up plenty of bait with just one sweep,
Catfish were everywhere, looking for something to eat.
Even the little ones were big enough to keep.
I was catching them so fast I didn't stop to eat

My reel got so hot I had to stick it in the creek.
This is the harvest I've been waiting to reap,
I had them all piled up in a great big heap,
Then my alarm clock went "beep-beep-beep!"
It was almost enough to make a grown man weep!
Being so rudely awakened from a nice, peaceful sleep,
And leave all those fish I know I can't keep.
But I'll be going back next time I go to sleep.
All this talk about fishing and the river
Is beginning to make my backbone shiver,
Goosebumps are breaking out, my liver is about to quiver,
Hook up the boat! I've got to get to the river!
But grab this thought and hold on to it tight,
If your mind is worried cause you ain't living right,
You better stay away from sandbars on Saturday night.
But if you are trying to do what's right,
You may dream your way to a Sandbar Saturday Night!
And maybe, that's what heaven really is like!

    For you non-fishermen, I'm going to go through this poem and point out how nearly every line contains vital information on stalking a catfish. You are on your own for the rest of the poems. Catfishing is a whole lot more than just a hobby. You can put meat on the table, or do it for a living, or for fun, or for the adrenaline rush. You have to be ready and willing to go when they are out hunting food, because I can't even catch them when they are not biting and I sure as hell am not going to stick my arms up in holes in the bank to doodle them. I've seen alligators longer than my boat and have caught snapping turtles so big they couldn't turn around in the bed of a pickup truck. I don't think running water will get hot enough to affect them, and some of my best catches were on cold nights when the bait would freeze to the boat seat in just a few minutes. Rain doesn't bother them because they can always get under the boat. It can drive you nuts, though, if you don't prepare for it.

As a rule, catfishing is generally more productive at night. There are several legal ways to catch catfish. You can stick poles in the bank or tie lines to overhanging branches, and the limb should be stiff enough to hook him; but limber enough to play him. You can also string out a long weighted line and attach a lot of short lines with baited hooks. This works well across rivers, creeks, sloughs, and lakes. Fish baskets made from cypress slats form a natural type habitat and catfish will sometimes go in just for cover, but a little stink bait helps.

No matter how you catch a catfish, he is going to put up a fight and stretch your string. A rod and reel is probably most popular and most exciting. A loaded pole is like mainlining adrenalin and cannot be properly described, but it keeps me going back, no matter how adverse the conditions. When everyone else is boarding and taping up their windows for a hurricane, I'm on the river, tying out bush hooks cause the river is going to come up for sure, and I don't want to miss out on that. It also doesn't matter how hard you have to work to be there when that magic little jerk happens, that makes all that disappear.

At the lower end of a sandbar is a good place to find big cats coming out of deep holes on the shallows, to feed on small fish which are less active after dark. It is no wonder that a small live bream is a good bait for big catfish. Sandbars are mostly wide-open, clear areas, which allow you plenty of room to let him run and wear himself down without many hangs and obstacles.

Anything over two reels and rods at a time is usually more trouble than it is worth. Catfish usually travel with other catfish and if you are fortunate enough to get two big ones on at the same time, you might O.D. Setting your poles out is very important. You may miss a lot of bites if there is too much slack in your line, and a big one can snatch your pole out of the boat before you can reach for it, unless it is tied down or in a good pole holder.

Catfish don't know which way the wind is blowing, or care how many clouds there are. They are sensitive to barometric pressures and the effect of the moon's gravity, though, so they do react to approaching fronts indicated by the amount of cloud cover, and to the position of the moon in the overhead sky. Millions of stars means no moon visible, and if you can see the moon, day or night, you might as well stay home till it sets, unless there are major overriding factors, like a sudden rise or fall of the river level or a mayfly hatch, or mussel kill due to dropping the river out suddenly. Evolution has not had time to catch up with man's ability to build dams and control water movements.

Catching or handling any size catfish can be dangerous, so be careful and stick to those soft drinks. You will get enough stimulation as soon as your rod tries to jump out of the boat. You will also have plenty of time between bites to contemplate the situation of your life and come up with some questions of your own, like the ones I have presented to you. In fishing, like in life, the outcome depends on the amount of preparation you have done and how responsible you are at covering all the aspects of all the tiny little conditions present, and those that might come up. If you don't get anything else out of this book, at least you will know how to catch supper.

I have visited over and over, several places in my dreams, like the one described in this poem. When I am there, they are real familiar, but when I am awake, I do not have a clue as to their location. So they are real to one part of my consciousness, and unknown to another part, which believes that the waking state is real, while the other part knows that it is not. This is part of the interplay between the spirit and ego. Wouldn't this also apply if you were permanently out of your body by death? So death and dreaming should be similar conditions experienced by the real me, who is doing the experiencing, so why not start practicing for death, during dreaming? Once you get out of your body, or should I say waking consciousness, no matter how you do it, all the rules change.

Things are no longer solid, and they can change with each thought. Time and space no longer exist, cause you can think your way to anywhere and anytime. You can walk on water or fly through the air, or fill your tackle box up with gold sinkers, hooks too. Maybe that is what heaven is like.

One day my fishing buddy and I were headed back in after fishing hard all morning with nothing to show for it. We had already been through every excuse we could think of as to why the fish weren't biting. We came flying into the little slough where we keep the boat, and scared a young, or nearsighted, osprey off a low limb of one of the huge trees that lined this little pond. He had apparently just caught this huge shad and barely made it to that low limb with it. He took off again with it, although it was all he could manage with both feet. He had to fly around the pond two times before he was able to gain enough altitude to clear the trees. On his fourth pass by the boat, my fishing buddy turned to me and said, "Look at that son-of-a-bitch pimping that fish!" Maybe she was more correct than I was, because I recognize that animals and birds also have their own little egos. He almost had more fish than he could carry, using only the equipment the Lord gave him. We had a boat with an outboard motor and a trolling motor and a depth machine with a fish finder, three tackle boxes, four or five reels and rods, two bream busters, a dip net, a gaff hook, two paddles, a hundred feet of rope, three anchors, three life jackets, a whistle, an extra can of gas, a bucket of minnows, a cage of crickets, two boxes of worms, a cup of stink bait, a half pound of shrimp, an ice chest full of drinks and snacks, an umbrella, and an empty live well. I don't blame him.

I know a whole lot more about fishing than I do about flying around the universe, so you will have to figure out TV analogy on your own. I like to have never got out of the yard and just made it out of the county.

CHAPTER FIVE
TV ANALOGY

I wasn't completely through with *Sandbar Saturday Night* and was still working hard for hours on end, polishing it up and balancing it and smoothing out the rough spots and arranging it in order. At one point I just got up from my desk and hobbled outside to get away from rhyming every thought, and get some sun and rest my mind. I had just sat down and started to shut down my mind for awhile, when suddenly I had to get up and get my notebook and pen. Brand new and totally alien thoughts in rhyme started flooding my mind. I wrote them down just as if I was taking dictation. That went on for awhile and when they stopped, I just put those papers away in my notebook without even paying any attention to what it said, because I was trying to take a break, and wanting to finish the catfish poem. I forgot all about the new poem until later the next day. Before daylight, though that next day, I woke up with poetry again gushing into my conscious mind. I turned on the light and got my notebook and sat there on the edge of my bed and wrote another poem as if by dictation. I didn't realize it till later, that it was a continuation of the poem I wrote the day before, and it fit together without a break. Spooky, ain't it!? The first thing they ask you at the crazy house, is, "Have you been hearing voices in your head?" It makes me wonder if all those crazy people are really crazy, or have they just been fooling with their tuning knob? I'll admit I have fooled around with mine. I can hardly tune in the world most of you inhabit most of the time, but before you get your net, you should hear what I heard.

TV ANALOGY

Doctors, healers, astronomers, astrologers, psychics, mystics, hypnotists,
exorcists, chemists, pharmacists, physicists, scientists, acupuncturists,
psychiatrists, biologists, geologists, meteorologists, cosmologists,
UFOolgosits, zoologists, ichthyologists, ornithologists, physiologists,
radiologists, neurologists, psychologists, theologists, ecologists,
seismologists, numerologists, archeologists, anthropologists,
and all the other ologists are beginning to agree
That this old world is nothing like what it seems to be.
After studying the facts, here is how it looks to me.
This world we know is not the real reality.
It is only one channel on cosmic TV
There are a zillion channel worlds here we don't even see!
We are surrounded by energy we cannot perceive,
For proof, just turn on your radio, cell phone, or TV.
Then sounds and pictures come out of the air magically
And for a new channel, just vary the frequency
Since our thoughts and body functions operate on electricity.
It makes good sense that it will work on you and me.
This is satellite earth channel Human Awake on Cosmic TV.
When we sleep, channel Human Dreaming is what we see.
When we die, channel Human Less Body is what we will be.
We grew up without a tuning knob, so this world is all we see.
And we're led to believe this is all there is to reality.
But no matter which channel we're on, we are still pure energy,
And that knowledge is the door that will set you free.
Perception is the lock and willpower is the key.
Leave yourself behind, and take off to infinity.
And roam the cosmic TV tuner throughout eternity,
Meditation is the on-off switch, volume is impeccability.
Love is the power supply, and fast-forward is prophecy.
On the VCR and rewind is our history's memory,
This Is Your Life is the tape that you will see.

The cable company is lucid dreaming, TV Guide is astrology,
There are no limits out there, they were all set here by me.
Some drugs change your channel, but just temporarily.
But you are playing roulette, you could easily get insanity.
A near-death experience can vary your frequency,
Your channel changes when you are out of your body.
And are still in view of the human awake eye, but it is unable to see.
You floating above your body, thinking which one is me.
Everything is different when you learn to erase,
This notion that you have about time and space
Reason always shows up and in first place!
Creating this idea of a solid world in every case,
But the world you know only exists behind your face
You process energy by what you see, touch and taste.
But you have extra sensory perception you will probably waste
You are a spark of the energy that is always every place.
But you let your mind and body severely limit that space.
And you waste your whole life hiding behind your face.
They have been trying to tell us about it ever since Eve,
But because of our self-importance, we are easy to deceive,
It is amazing the amount of stuff we were led to believe.
We will buy just about any idea anybody can conceive,
And end up with everything except the one we need.

    You are not your body. That is the most important information that a human being can know. All the outstanding people who ever existed knew that, and tried to explain it to everyone else in their own way. Now there is plenty of data to prove it, but it is essential that everyone finds that out for themselves. If you don't learn that in this lifetime, you will know it for sure when your heart makes its final beat and you look at that dead body and realize you are still alive. Then you will also know that all the ideas you have ever had, based on sensory perception, are no longer valid. Your body, along with everything else, which is also energy or mass, depending on the speed of its vibration or the amount of materials in the object, is created by perceiving energy at various frequencies through visual, audible, touch, smell, and taste receptors, and running them through the brain. The read-out is our view of the world, and only at that particular frequency of energy can our world be found. We did not include the frequencies outside our sensory range as part of our world until we developed a method of detecting them. So, now with x-ray machines and ultraviolet lights and radar, radios and TVs and cell phones, we can incorporate them into our life and prove that they are there, even though the body, without the devices, can't detect them.

Therefore, because of the limited view of energy our bodies have, all of us learned by the same process of growing up to perceive it and label it, so that we could communicate about it, and we were led to an erroneous conclusion of reality. That confusion is the basic cause of all the diversities of behavior in human history. Each body perceives itself as a separate entity, instead of a component part of total awareness, which we all are on all levels, other than the physical. Therefore, all behavior that we label as hostile or unjust or destructive or sinful, originates from not being aware that we are all parts of the whole thing, and by not knowing that, if we mistreat the other parts of everything, we are at the same time mistreating ourselves.

Ego is the term most people have adopted to label the physical material portion of our consciousness, that we call I, but I found out when I first became aware of being separated from my body, that the real me was awake and perceiving in a different way from usual, while I was asleep in my bed, a few hundred yards away. In other words, I woke up outside my body. How do I know that it wasn't a dream? It doesn't matter, because if you are not in your body, a dream is just as real as the everyday world is to you, when you are in your body. They are both just thought forms vibrating at different speeds.

Another good reason is because I had been consciously trying to get out of my body for a long time. Ever since I had heard about it, which is called astral projection, from a book by a Tibetan monk who had to flee the Chinese invasion. I had been using a technique from a book by an anthropologist who had become an apprentice to an old Indian man of knowledge, who had wisdom obtained and added to for many, many generations through an apprenticeship, of discipline, responsibility, hands-on manipulation of awareness, ingestion of psychotropic plants and the breaking down of the ego's description of the world. There is a lot of ancient information showing up that makes some of our foremost scholars look like first graders.

If you interpret the Bible correctly, you will also find that its basic truth also contains directions to separate the body from the spirit. Jesus taught Peter how to shift from ego to spirit consciousness, allowing him to also walk on water, thus defying the universal laws of gravity upon which everything in the physical universe is based. Peter was successful until his ego's reason convinced him that this was not possible and that caused his vibration to shift back to the physical level where indeed, it is not possible, and Peter began to sink. It had nothing to do with Jesus and his ability to sustain the spiritual vibration in himself.

After being out of my body awhile and knowing something wasn't quite right, but not realizing exactly what it was, I looked at my hands as I had suggested in the waking state as the first step upon finding myself awake in a dream. The shock I experienced from realizing that I had spent nearly three decades of my life in an illusion created by my senses, was nearly more than I could stand, and it sent me flying through the air and through the roof of my bedroom and around the room before I finally settled back into my body without a break in conscious awareness. I was no longer depending on faith. I knew for sure then and there that I was not my body. I haven't been the same person since that day, and it took years for me to get over that shock enough to get out of my body again. That is probably why it is so difficult to do, because we must have a built-in mechanism to prevent it from happening before we are spiritually prepared to do so. I no longer try to do it, but every

73

now and then it just happens, and I enjoy it more and more every time, now that I possess considerably more spiritual energy than I had then.

Physicists have determined that nothing can go faster than the speed of light, but at the same time they say that the universe expanded a million, million, million, million, million times in just a fraction of a second. I haven't done the math, but that sounds like a contradiction to me. Could they be wrong about that, too? My point is, that no matter how you perceive the universe, whether it is by telescope or microscope, it is still being filtered through the human eyeball and brain frequency of energy, and will look about the same, however you observe it. I've never once heard any of them wondering if all those other bands of energy, including radio frequency energy bands, could actually be the other worlds they are looking for and can't find, because they don't have a correct frequency eyeball brain receiver to turn it into the world it also is. That could be the dark matter that they know is there, but don't have the means to access and locate it, and it is as close as the end of their antennae.

So that indicates that just the ideas based on spirit are the only ones that are actually valid. If you were willing and able to look at God for a minute from a physical point of view rather than a religious of your choice point of view, and change God's name to energy, you would find that all the pieces of the puzzle fit perfectly into that model that would make us all sparks off of that energy that is always every place. It takes us all to make up the whole, so it becomes very easy to understand why it is necessary to love thy neighbor.

If you had been born blind and remained that way all your life, there is no way that anyone could describe red to you, no matter how long or hard they tried. You still would not even have a clue to what they were trying to communicate. But suppose you were able to see red for just one second? Then you would know what red is, but you still would not be able to describe it to anyone else. That same principle applies to all energy outside the normal range of human perception. Therefore you can experience spirit and learn to perceive energy outside the range of normal humans, but you cannot properly describe it to someone else. To know about it then, means that you have to experience it and to experience it you must locate your tuning knob and adjust the frequency of your mind, to be compatible with the frequency you are seeking.

To do so may be the result of natural progression of spiritual growth, from applying loving and caring and responsibility principals to your life, no matter what name you call God. It also happens regularly in the dream state we occupy nightly, but because of sensorial interpretations by the body consciousness, it is usually disregarded and left unavailable to us to utilize if we are able to even recognize it at all. Through practice, though, you can create a conduit to spiritual energy through dreaming. Your body needs sleep to maintain itself, but the higher portions of your consciousness that are not directly involved with the body functions, do not require rest and are therefore free to roam the universe, as energy unfettered by time or space. Retrieving that information only comes from returning to that state consciously, or by merging the two consciousnesses into the total self. The better you become at handling energy, and the more you demonstrate the proper intentions, the more energy is channeled to you and through you, and the by-product is spiritual bliss, and is your reward.

There are some drugs and plants that can alter your perception centers that can also allow you some spiritual awareness, but they can also drive you insane or kill you, if you are not tuned in correctly. So be sure you are ready to handle altered states before you ever even try to induce them, because you might succeed. I am sure that about everybody has heard about bad trips, but you don't know shit until you have had one, and lived through it. You won't be in a hurry to try it again. I will guarantee that!

Accidents which cause trauma to the brain have also caused cases of perception changes in some individuals. One of the most powerful psychometrists around awoke from a coma after falling off a ladder three stories up, with the ability to obtain personal information from someone by merely holding on to their keys or other items on which their vibrations had come in contact. Near-death and death resuscitation experiences always begin with the victim floating out of their body and realizing they don't identify the body as themselves, but as just their body. Then while out of the body, they can observe everything going on around them, but no one else is aware that even though they are right there, no one sees them. They often encounter friends or relatives who are dead, who are now of a compatible frequency, due to the loss of the influence of the body. Next, they usually encounter positive energy from the new perspective, unfiltered by the body's senses, and describe it as light and love and joy and peace. Then, they see their whole life, no matter how many years old they are, flash by in seconds. How does that compute on your space-time continuum? Does the spiritual energy go out into space, however many years, and isolate your light energy and then follow it back at near-light speed to the present, in order to show you all the mistakes you have made? Must be something like that, because nearly all those who make it back tell a similar story, and usually all of them begin a completely spiritual path without much more hindrance from the ego.

There are many cases reported of patients showing up with multiple personalities, some with over a hundred, whose blood test, urinalysis, EKGs, etc., register different readings from the same body, depending on which personality is "out". Some of the personalities are male, some female, some are old and some are young. Some have exceptional skills or destructive behavior. All of them are different, with different identities, which seem to be shattered parts of the dominant one. This doesn't fit our old ideas as to one personality to one body, but there it is. Then, what about hypnosis? Patients have gone through root canals under hypnosis and no anesthesia, with no pain. People have gone through regressive hypnosis back in time, to other lives and returned with new knowledge that can be traced back to that time. Some have even reported on lifetimes that are in the future. This is not bullshit. There are tons of evidence to back up these cases.

These things won't go into a physical model but they fit perfectly into an energy one. Maybe that is why, if you stop the internal dialogue by hypnosis or meditation or dreaming, it allows direct access to spiritual energy that is not dampened by the body.

If you ask why should anyone care about this now, instead of just waiting till your body dies and experiencing it naturally, I would cite Mozart as an example in reverse. In order to write concertos at the age of three, he obviously brought musical knowledge to his new body from another dimension of consciousness, which preceded his birth. Likewise, you can carry knowledge learned in this dimension, into the energy body you inhabit after death. So, instead of fearing death, you can begin to learn how to function again in that state and to prepare yourself for that glorious trip to freedom from isolation. A positively-charged spirit will help keep the negative aspects of universal energy from becoming a hell.

The choice is yours. Are you a part of the planet that respects every other part as equal, and an asset to the whole, or are you like a cancer that is willing to kill off your host organism through your own selfishness and greed and ignorance? God does not send you to hell for punishment. Negative charges seek negativeness just as positive charges are the consequences of positiveness.

The dollar bill is probably the most negative influence that has ever been perpetuated on humanity. Hell will be full to the brim with rich folks and poor folks trying anything under the sun to be rich. Little do they realize that cash, checks, or credit cards are not accepted at the Pearly Gates. The only luggage they do accept is in the form of spiritual knowledge. Where the best bargains are and how to cheat on your taxes or how to con or rip off others or how to make money pillaging the earth, is not going to be any help when your heart stops ticking, and it is going to stop one of these days.

Most people do not realize that before their body was born and after it dies, the spark of awareness that is actually you, existed in a totally different environment. You can't remember it, or how totally helpless you were for so long after birth. During that time your ego began creating a physical world out of energy and gradually you forgot, or didn't learn, to access your spiritual nature in the new body. You still have that spiritual body, but when ego mingles with other egos, the characteristics of the physical are generally dominant and rule behavior. Your spiritual side, which is not a slave to time and space, was aware of what the consequences of your life was going to be, and had input into the type body and environment you would need to perform the task you came into the physical to do. Well, if that is the case, why didn't everybody choose a perfect body and situation to be in? They did, but perfect has a vastly different meaning to the ego.

Suppose your charge was very negative due to how you used it in the past, and you could only afford the very cheapest model body available to get a chance to become positive? Hell gets old after awhile. Heaven and hell are the opposite ends of the same energy spectrum. You might have to take a pretty horrible body if you don't have much energy to spend. Most of the horrible bodies are kept out of normal view or are worked on in sometimes brutal ways, to make them conform to the ego mind's status quo.

I had the opportunity to witness a perfect example of what I'm trying to say, while I was working in a facility for the severely retarded. Two clients, about middle age, had very similar conditions. Their IQ's were barely measurable and neither was able to communicate with anyone. Both had physical deformities and were handicapped to the max. One was confined to an oversized baby bed because his only limited body movement was spasmodic.

The other client could sit in a wheelchair and could only move one arm, which had to be kept tied down most of the time because the only thing he did with it was to beat himself in the head. He screamed all day long, every day of his life. The other client in the baby bed with almost identical conditions never screamed or cried or beat himself. He laughed and cooed and squealed like any happy baby would, all the time. To me this represents a perfect example of heaven and hell.

Hell is being caught in an undeveloped physical and mental body with an undeveloped spiritual body. Heaven is being able to be happy in any undeveloped physical and mental body, because of a developed spiritual body. So, if you don't start now developing your spiritual self, you too may be severely handicapped when your body dies and you find yourself in spirit form, no matter how many times you got saved at church.

Today we have neurosurgeons who can prod certain areas of the human brain with magnetic devices, and seem to create all kinds of mental images, including memories or feelings of an alien abduction. Lots of UFO incidents are recorded near known magnetic aberrations. So this looks bad for the UFO researchers until you realize that the neurosurgeon cannot be sure his devices did not alter the frequencies of the perception centers, thus allowing them to indeed tune in alien energy. Look what happens when you get your microphone, which is a magnetic device, too close to your speakers. You can then get all kinds of foreign sounds, from an electronic sound system in perfect working order. Our brains work on electrical signals very much like TVs and computers.

Speaking of computers, technology now advances as much per day as it did per decade before the computer. Humans now have the ability to do almost anything that can be thought up. We now have accurate computer models of the universe, weather systems, DNA, atomic particles, and practically everything else. They already know how to alter the genetic structure of almost every living thing so that they can create designer organisms. They say that bodies of the future will be partially robotic and designed for whatever situation they will be used in. Science fiction is rapidly becoming science fact, that is, if we don't blow ourselves up first, or kill our planet before we can escape it.

One more thing about bodies for you racists and homophobes. The spiritual body is not male or female. It's not black or white, or red or oriental, or Jewish. It just is. It has always been and has been all of the above at some time or other. So, if you hate blacks, or honkies, or fags, it is probably that you were one in a recent lifetime. Get over it or you might be one next time, too.

There is no such thing as security on the physical planet earth, with asteroids constantly crossing our path, natural disasters, war, disease, pollution, terrorists, old age, and now even paparazzi. The Princess, with all her wealth, fame, influence, and a team of personal bodyguards, was killed in a car crash. How often do you ride in a car?

I guess I'm through now. I have passed on the wisdom and knowledge that I have compiled from what I have learned from experience and from others along the path that has helped me so much on my present journey through the earth plane at this most exciting and momentous time in human evolution. I'm not going to try to tell anyone how to live. There are already plenty of qualified teachers out there who have already covered that topic thoroughly in many different ways. Happiness is available and it is your choice, but it requires action, and dethroning an out-of-control ego can be a very difficult task, but thank goodness you can get an equal or more amount out of it than you put into it.

I have probably offended many organized religions and governments, although that was not my main intention. My concern is, however, that religion and politics have always felt it necessary to control other people's minds and influence their behavior. I am not sure that is their job, unless they can demonstrate it by their own actions.

I have borrowed a few phrases and words from other writers throughout this book. I did not do it to capitalize on their work. I did it out of respect for their work.

So! The answer to the question *"Was I a Poet and Didn't Know It?"* will have to be decided by you. My guess is, maybe. One of my best friends might have best summed it all up by saying, "Maybe you just had a bad case of verbal diarrhea." Could be. At least I quit writing in rhymes. So, look forward to my sequel, "Was I an Author and Didn't Know It?"

CHAPTER SIX
DIFFERENT WAYS OF LOOKING AT SAME THING

Apparently I was wrong in thinking that I had quit writing in rhymes, because as I was doing the first final rewrite on this book, I started receiving some lines on what has become my favorite poem yet, and I just had to include it in this book. I think I was just kidding about my sequel. It is about perception and I would like to make it into a children's book later, although it is good for adults, too.

This poem started coming in one afternoon while I was babysitting my grandson. It had been over 30 years since I had been around any kids long enough to notice how fast they pick up knowledge and develop communication skills, and how energetically they engage in exploring their brand new environment. I had become very interested in how our minds had described our world to us as various objects and wondered how babies, who had to start from scratch, by turning each energy pattern into an object, perceive the world. I also wondered the same thing about all the other forms of life with such a vast array of different kinds of sensory organs. There is absolutely no way that each different species of life can perceive planet earth the way humans do, and so therefore, humans and other species create their own description of the world. That should easily convince anyone that there are, indeed, many, many layers of frequency that are missing from the human point of view, and the human point of view is as diverse as the amount of different cultures we have sprung from.

When anthropologists started documenting behaviors of different, isolated groups of people, they found that everyone in a particular tribe, that altered their basic body in some form of tattooing, piercing, scarring or stretching, all did the same thing.

There were no stretched necks in a tribe with alligator scars, or no tattoos on those who had stretched lips. Likewise, the whole group had common ideas about God and nature and behavior, no matter how different it was from those across the river, continent, or globe.

Now, after years of social mingling, there are hardly any unique tribes left. They have been so cross-cultured for so long that you are likely to find any kind of body disfiguring or ideas on religion or behavior anywhere in the world. I have often wondered what the first human was thinking about when he picked up a nail and said, "I wonder how I would look with this sticking through my nose or ear lobe or nipple?" After the first ones did it, it wasn't too hard to get others interested. Humans can be led so easily to do almost anything. They would often do it to their kids, too, so naturally, their kids wanted to do it to their kids. Same thing with religion and other behavior. So now about every culture can look at any of the others and say, "Now ain't that a stupid thing to do or say." Just imagine two native Africans standing under a cow's upraised tail waiting for her to piss on them, for insect repellent, and talking about those crazy Americans, and how many different religions they have. So if we are all dummies to everyone else, then we must all really be dumb. So what are we going to do about it? How are we going to break the cycle by massing all the children into huge school systems so they can all get the same education with equal parts of brainwashing and negative behavior traits thrown in? Then the marketing guys on TV will take over when they get home and convince them they just have to have all the proper brand-name junk they dish out, or they won't fit in. It is no wonder that so many kids are into drugs and gangs and guns and killing other kids. What are the government agencies, who are responsible for social order, going to do when those kids find out who the real oppressors are?

All I know that can be done is to set a good example in your own behavior and try to educate your kids in awareness of the positive spiritual side of consciousness. In order to do this, though, perception is the first nut you have to crack, before you can feed on the rest. If you don't accept that our so-called "real world" is just one of the possibilities, then you sure can't achieve any of the others.

That is why I'm so happy to share this next poem with you, because to me it helps show you how to go about thinking about solving the perception problem. I can trace the first line of that poem that came into my mind one day out of the blue sky, in rhyme, back to a day about three months earlier, when my brother's dog jumped out of the boat on to an island while we were fishing. We had been talking about perception and I said then, as he was sniffing all around, that he was just looking around. With the number of big alligators around there where I fish, it makes it essential for a dog to hit new ground with his nose to the ground to keep from being supper for a big gator, who can hide in just a few inches of water. Some ole boys around here got to losing some of their high-priced hunting dogs, and finally traced one of their beeping collars to the belly of a ten-foot gator. There were thirteen collars, three of them still beeping, in that gator. When the line about the dog came in, I wrote it in my notebook where I recorded incoming bits of information. The line directly above it, which had come in a couple of months earlier, was different ways of looking at the same thing, and it just happened to be the perfect title for that new poem. Coincidence? I don't think so. When you get on down the path, that is the way things start happening. If you need something, it just shows up.

DIFFERENT WAYS OF LOOKING AT THE SAME THING

Dog went outside to look around
And stuck his nose down to the ground.
Bat said, "Dog, that is not the way to see
I'll show you how, just look at me."
The bat let out a shriek and wiggled his ear.
Dog said, "No, Bat, that's how you hear."
A fly flew by and stopped and said,
"I can look all the way around without moving my head.
I can read your lips from far or near
But it is hard to hear without an ear."
Lizard said, "That's nothing, so can I!
I can see half at a time with either eye!
And even though I don't have much of an ear,
I heard you coming before you got here."
Dog said, "I can see you moving night or day
But to recognize you, I can't be very far away.
But if I look around with my nose to the ground,
I know who can be found on this side of town.
And my ears are tuned to the slightest sound,
With them I know who is on the other side of town."
Pigeon said, "Dog, that is mere child's play
I can see who is in town from ten miles away.
And if I didn't mind flying night and day,
I could go back home either way."
Seagull said, "I could fly across the ocean
But I get dizzy looking at all that motion.
So I dive in the water and look around,
To see if there are any little fish to be found."
Eagle said, "I can see a fish ten feet deep
From two miles high but I catch them with my feet.
So before I dive I have to know
If it's a little one near the top, or a big one down below."

Bat said, "I can see where there is no light
So I can live in a cave and hunt at night.
I see better with my ears than I do with my eyes
Nothing hides from me no matter how dark the skies."
Owl said, "I also do a lot of my hunting at night,
My feathers are designed for silent flight,
And they make a dish around my eyes and ears,
So that each eye sees just what it hears."
Earthworm said, "I don't need eyes cause I live underground.
But I still know when its night and I go out crawling around."
Sunflower said, "I don't have an eye and I don't need one,
But you will always find my face looking at the sun."
"Sunflower, what you do sounds a lot like me.
I even fold my leaves up tight at night," said the mimosa tree.
Potato said, "I've got eyes but I can't see,
I use them to make new copies of me."
About that time up walked a man.
He said, "I can see better than all of you can."
They all laughed and said, "Is this a joke?"
Then he pulled out a telescope.
Just one look at his truck revealed many things,
From a radar scope to an x-ray machine.
He had night vision goggles with a wide-angle lens,
And he went back to his truck again and again.
With binoculars, a microscope, and a satellite dish,
Will this all soon be over? was everyone's wish.
"While you were unloading we all voted, and agree
Sure takes a lot of stuff for you to be able to see!
Since my flight blows the mind of your aircraft industry,
I was elected spokesman by the whole community.
To deliver this challenge to you," said the bumblebee.
"My sight is not in the range of your visual frequency,
So we would all like to watch you, try to see,
Just how beautiful a sunset looks to me.
Got you again! Tee hee, tee hee."

Through modern medical technology, it is now possible to fix some problems which had caused blindness, in some cases all the way back to birth, but they discovered that even though the patients could see with 20/20 vision, their sight was absolutely useless and was a considerable hindrance to their usual ability to get around, through the use of the other senses. They were able to observe patterns of light and color, but those patterns had never been identified or named or run through the brain, eyeball perception process, so that every aspect of seeing had to be learned from scratch before sight was of any use to them. Hold your thumb out at arm's length and with both eyes open, line your thumb up with a distant object. Now, without moving your thumb, look at that alignment with one eye and then with the other. Notice how the alignment doesn't change with one eye, but it shifts over considerably with the other? So, one is in error, and you may have never even noticed it before, but that and depth perception and other seemingly insignificant things made it almost impossible to learn to see. So, unfortunately, most of the patients chose to be blind again, because it was so difficult to use the new sense without sometimes years of learning to see. Of all the fascinating facts of life, humans of Earth find that focusing on the visual formations of matter, are of most importance to the assimilation of knowledge. Stop here and reread out loud that last sentence. Okay, now count how many times the letter F was present in that statement. Stop again. If you think it showed up six times, count them again. You were only half right. There are actually 12 F's there. This time, your brain lied to you, because it was still in reading mode which saw "of" as "ov" and therefore, missed counting the F's in of. That again proves that you can't believe everything you see. Have you ever seen a mirage? Your eyeball brain connections are then telling you that you are seeing something that is not there at all!

All your senses can fool you. If you live or work near a paper mill or oil refinery, your brain will get so tired of the smell that you will actually quit smelling it. If you live by a railroad track or a barking dog long enough, you will quit hearing them, but if you hear three or four notes, unannounced, to the National Anthem, you will automatically stand up. I worked in an electric shop one time that had an old supply room. Twenty years later I again walked into that supply room and remembered exactly how it smelled and I believe I could have picked it out of a million supply rooms. A dog could have picked it out of a trillion. A dog can smell where you were weeks ago, but he can't see you well enough to identify you more than a few feet away. The Navy used pigeons in search and rescue because a pigeon can see an orange life preserver 13 miles away. A human can barely see an aircraft hangar at half that distance. There is not much chance that this world is going to look the same to me as it does to the dog or the pigeon.

The reason I keep going over and over this, is because it is so important and extremely hard to picture in our mind. Most people today have indoor plumbing and electricity in their home and use both all the time. Nine out of ten people understand basic plumbing because you can stand at your sink, and see that the water coming in, comes from a small pipe because it is under pressure. You can tell how much water is there by how deep it gets in the sink. They also know that to get rid of all that water, the drain pipe must be much larger than the feed pipe, because with no pressure, the water is only removed by gravity, thus taking longer to drain than to fill.

An ole boy told my brother one day that all you need to know about electricity is that there is a positive and a negative, but he wasn't positive which one was negative. Well, it is a whole lot more complicated than that and you can spend four years in college studying it and still not be sure you understand all you know about it.

I have already taught you how to fish so I'm going to show you how to understand basic electricity, by comparing the actions of electrons in a circuit to water in your pipe. The only thing that nine out of ten people know about electricity, is that it will knock the shit out of you. They have no idea what an ohm, or a volt, or an amp, or a watt is. In 30 seconds, I'm going to teach you basic electricity by comparing those terms to their counterparts in plumbing. An ohm measures resistance to electron flow just like the size of a pipe resists water flow. A volt is the pressure of the electron flow just like the PSI pressure is to the water flow. An amp is the amount of electrons flowing in the circuit, just like the amount of water in the plumbing pipes. A watt is the measurement of the total electricity used just like the amount of water in the sink. Now, see how easy that was to understand? You could compare it to something tangible.

I think I have come up with a way to compare the workings of the non-tangible ego-spirit-body operation with a tangible, although complicated, example, to give you an idea as to how to think about this consciousness relationship. Believe me, I know how hard it is to get a handle on this consciousness operation. I used to say that we are the whole ocean but our ego makes us just a single drop, but that is way too simple.

Most sophisticated airplanes have an autopilot, and most sophisticated autopilots have a function which allows pilots to fly the autopilot, while the autopilot is flying the airplane. In other words, the human pilot in preparation for the trip, puts the coordinates for altitude, course and speed into the autopilot's computer and takes off. The autopilot detects any variation of this information's proposed flight plan, and essentially corrects itself at the same rate of deviation, so that plane goes where it should at the proper speed and altitude. This is very helpful to the pilot. Now suppose there were some unscheduled obstacles in his path such as thunderstorms, air traffic, flock of birds, or UFO. Whatever the case, the pilot could fly the autopilot around or over the situation and then allow the autopilot to take back over control and correct for the deviation without having to plot and crank in new coordinates, or otherwise disturbing the autopilot. This is also very helpful to the pilot.

Now, let's imagine that your body is the airplane and your ego is the autopilot, and your spirit is the pilot. Get the picture? Okay. The spirit (pilot) plots the course and details of the trip and turns control of the body (airplane) over to the ego (autopilot) who remains in control for the duration of life (trip), unless obstacles are encountered. If you have a good, calibrated, properly working ego or autopilot, you can sit back and enjoy the trip.

Unfortunately, sometimes things go wrong with autopilots and egos. Tiny little things can cause disasters. Let us suppose that you are planning a trip and have to cross some 10,000 feet tall mountains near the ocean at night, so you set your altitude for 15,000 feet, then you get a small leak in the line which supplies outside barometric pressure to the altimeter and autopilot reference. Leaks happen all the time. The equivalent problem in a person's ego could be something as simple as wanting a new pickup, or doublewide trailer, or bass boat. In the airplane both the altimeter and the autopilot reference are going to be gradually changing to cabin pressure of 5,000 feet, so the autopilot starts trying to correct to 15,000 feet where it already was. No matter how steep it climbs or high it flies, it cannot maintain, so it could either stall or exceed ceiling limits for that particular type aircraft and have an engine quit. Sounds bad, but it wouldn't be much of a problem for a good alert pilot. It wouldn't take him long to notice the difference between the altimeter and the autopilot setting, and he could disengage the autopilot and manually climb or descend and know there was an error in his altimeter. Then he could take proper precaution, even though he still doesn't know his true altitude, and could descend into the mountains or exceed ceiling limits. At least he has his parachute handy in case the problem gets too serious. The pilot (spirit) is safe, but poor autopilot (ego) has to go down with the airplane (body). Pilots (spirit) can always get new planes (bodies) with autopilots (egos). That is about as simple as I can make it.

Egos kill off bodies regularly when the spirit ain't flying the body around obstacles. Have you ever had a close call in which you escaped some tragedy against all odds, or have you ever done something so stupid you can't figure out why you did it, or something like that? That was just an alert spirit flying your ego into or out of a situation that was unscheduled, but necessary, without disturbing your awareness so that you would still get to the pre-arranged destination no matter how many detours your ego took. Don't forget that the pilot can turn off the autopilot any time he wants to and can fly the plane himself. The autopilot doesn't have that option. Now, is that too difficult to understand? The difficult part is shutting down ego, because it knows all the tricks to survival and it is stupid enough to self-destruct, taking the body down with it. It happens all the time. Suicides, drug overdoses, mountain climbing, cave diving or bull riding. There is a very fine line between bravery and stupidity, but if you can ride the bull, you can wear the buckle.

If you can regain control from the ego, you can do anything, anytime, anywhere. Good luck and remember that your results equal exactly how much you put into your goals, so don't expect a change in your life if you are not willing to change your behaviors, and you must share more than one-half of your energy or you are operating in the deficit column. Don't forget that you can't get full credit for energy expended on family and friends, because if they were not important to your ego, they might not get anything, either.

Don't make the mistake of confusing morality with spirituality. Would we have all been born naked if God required us to wear clothes? Would Jesus have turned water into wine if we were all supposed to be teetotalers? One of the world's leading authorities on psychotropic plants that humans have used throughout history and all over the globe, said that if it had not been for the psilocybin mushroom that early man found growing only out of the cow turds of wandering herds, that humans would not have come down out of the trees to follow them around.

Imagine that. If you eat one of them you will have no trouble understanding that there is more than you could ever guess possible to us as beings of perception. Scientists have hooked up machines to track brain activity of persons under the influence of these "magic mushrooms," and could actually see the enormous amount of signals being processed, as opposed to "normal brains." Normal brains don't hear colors or see sounds or even comprehend the possibility of such a concept. Normal brains have been so conditioned to the pinned-down description of the "real world" that when someone tells of a unique or unusual experience, they always preface it with "you might think I'm crazy, but this really happened." So if you ever had a ghost or UFO encounter, or saw Big Foot, or experienced any kind of extra-sensory perception from telepathy to clairvoyance, or had any contact from the dead or past lives, or near-death resuscitations, or any other out of the body experiences, or witnessed accurate prophecies, or dreams of events before they actually happened, then you will be thought of as crazy by the normal, or should I say abnormal, brains of humans. I would venture to say that nowadays more people have experienced one or more of those types of phenomena than people who have not. We are coming out of Pisces and into Aquarius, which is known as the Age of Enlightenment.

We have just gone over the six billion mark of humans on earth, and no two are exactly alike. Have you ever looked through the Book of World Records? What is normal? Who is normal? The only opinion that matters is your own. It is the only one that you have any control over, unless you honor agreements that you did not participate in. If that is your case, then you may as well forget making any progress on your road to happiness, because your life will always be dictated by forces beyond your control, and that is what you get.

So, for those of you who are not totally satisfied with your life, I'm going to reveal the secret to success. Change what you can and accept the rest. You are what you think and only you can keep yourself from singing yourself a happy song.

CHAPTER SEVEN
HOW TO DO IT

STEP 1.

Inventory your mind. Where did all the important beliefs that you live by originate? Have they been validated by investigation and scrutiny by you, or is it just what you have been taught all your life?

STEP 2.

Make a list of just the beliefs that you have, that you know to be 100% true.

STEP 3.

Make another list of beliefs you have, but are not certain that they are true.

STEP 4.

Start running all decisions and choices and points of view through items in Step 2.

STEP 5.

Start trying to move the items in Step 3 into Step 2, through open-minded investigation. Discard untrue beliefs when proven wrong.

STEP 6.

Inventory your possessions and make a list of everything you really, really do need. Make another list of everything else. This will give you an honest weigh-in on the size of your ego.

STEP 7.

Make a list of all the things you want but do not yet have.

STEP 8.

Start reducing items in second column of Step 6 and items in Step 7.

STEP 9.

Inventory your behavior. List positive traits in Column A and negative traits in Column B.

STEP 10.

Start moving items into Column A and remove items out of Column B.

STEP 11.

Inventory and list all your fears.

STEP 12.

Inventory and list all your worries.

STEP 13.

Inventory and list all your prejudices.

STEP 14.

Get rid of all the items in Steps 11, 12, and 13. You won't be needing any of them.

STEP 15.

Inventory your time. If you are not spending at least 51% on spirit, by helping others or working on these steps for yourself, you are going backwards on your path. You don't get something from nothing. I told you before that it takes a lot of work to get spirit back in control of your body. NOW is all you have. The past is gone, so let go of it. The future ain't here yet, so stop living for it, because it may not ever arrive for you.

STEP 16.

Inventory your relationships. Do you use your spouse or parents or children or friends for your own gain, or do you allow them to be their own selves and accept them for what they are? Like the man said, "Men and women are from different planets." Do not expect a happy love life if you found some hunk or babe and intend to change the few little bad characteristics they have. They don't change and they don't quit bitching when you don't change. Straighten up your own act and when you can be happy on your own and not dependent on anyone else for happiness, then you will attract people with the same qualities and are guaranteed successful relationships. It was only a little while after I consciously decided to quit looking for a companion, till the perfect one showed up.

STEP 17.

Inventory your body parts. If your feet are too long, so what? It is better than having no feet at all. This body is a reflection of your energy and it is your residence on the physical plane this trip. If you are not proud of it, that is just too bad. Look around you and see what some people got. So before you start altering it to fit your style, you better be sure the new style fits your spirit.

STEP 18.

Inventory your mission. Were you put here on earth to consume your ass off? I doubt it, but that seems to be everyone's goal, and look what is happening to Mother Earth. Do your part to help her out.

STEP 19.

Inventory your religious beliefs. If your religion is working for you, then stick with it, cause you are already happy and free from worry and fear, and you don't need any advice from me. If it is not working, then you really don't believe in it, anyway. I believe that if religion was valid, there could only be one. If you are making your living off of it, I don't think you really understand it, and if you mislead people with it, you will be held accountable for it. If there were no obstacles in your path, there would be no need to make the trip. Stop and think what would your religion be if you were born in Russia, or Iran, or China, or Mexico, or a rain forest, or an Eskimo village, or an Indian reservation, or Salt Lake City?

STEP 20.

Inventory your political beliefs. Nowadays the candidate who can raise the most money usually wins. Is that a good way to select a leader? If your participation is only as simple as voting, be aware that you are just as guilty of bombing a target as the man who made the bomb and the pilot who flew the mission, because your vote helped elect the people who gave the order. Hitler alone is not responsible for murdering millions of Jews. The millions of Germans who allowed him to have that kind of control are just as guilty. Same thing with gun control. Don't blame the gun for doing its job. Blame the idiot who pulled the trigger. You would think that by now the people making the laws would have figured out that you can't legislate behavior. You can only hold people responsible for their actions. Just exactly what is it about a job that pays a few hundred thousand dollars, that requires you to raise a few million dollars to get? What do those contributions get you? Is it a good idea to have a secret government, with federal, state, county and military police? It is your tax money that is financing this farce. Shouldn't you have some input into how it is used? Well, you don't. So if your president blows up the world don't complain about it because whether you voted for him or not, he was still elected by votes, that is if you believe your vote makes any difference. It didn't this last time, did it? Anyway, your leaders are responsible for the way things are. If you are not satisfied, you are shit out of luck. Get over it. If you connect to spirit you won't give a shit what they do.

STEP 21.

Now that you have thoroughly looked at your life, you and only you know what areas need work and how much. If you want to know what you can do to make a difference, I will tell you. It is so simple, yet so vastly important. No one can change anyone else, but if you just change yourself toward spirit, you will have done your part. Just maybe someone will notice and want to follow your example.

LAST STEP.

If any of the things I presented in this book have helped you on your road to happiness, I request that you don't stick this book in your bookcase to gather dust. When you are through with it, please look around and see if you can find another dummy who is dumb enough to read it and pass it on.

Thanks and Happy Trails to You!

THE END

Love, Love, Love – everything lovable!
Laugh, Laugh, Laugh – at everything else.